CONFLUENCE

A River, The Environment, Politics, & The Fate of All Humanity

NATHANIEL TRIPP

Foreword by Howard Dean

STEERFORTH PRESS
Hanover, New Hampshire

In memory of Rachel Carson

Copyright © 2005 by Nathaniel Tripp

LIBRARY OF CONGRESS CATALOGING-IN-PUBLICATION DATA
Tripp, Nathaniel, 1944–
Confluence : a river, the environment, politics, and the fate of all
humanity / Nathaniel Tripp.— 1st ed.
p. cm.
Includes bibliographical references and index.
ISBN 1-58642-088-7 (alk. paper)
1. Connecticut River — Description and travel. 2. Connecticut River
— History. 3. Natural history — Connecticut River. 4. Connecticut
River — Environmental conditions. 5. Environmental protection —
Connecticut River. 6. Water — Pollution — Connecticut River.
7. Connecticut River — Regulation. I. Title.

F12.C7T75 2005
974—DC22

2004030177

FIRST EDITION

Acknowledgments

I wish to thank the residents of the Connecticut Valley, especially those who worked long days in the fields, forests, the industries and the communities and then put in long evenings on management plans. Thanks also to Adair Mulligan, and those long late drives; to Howard Dean who showed the way, on the river as at the conference table; and especially to Sharon Francis, whose insight and leadership inspires so many.

And finally, a special thanks to Chip Fleischer, once again. Thanks Chip!

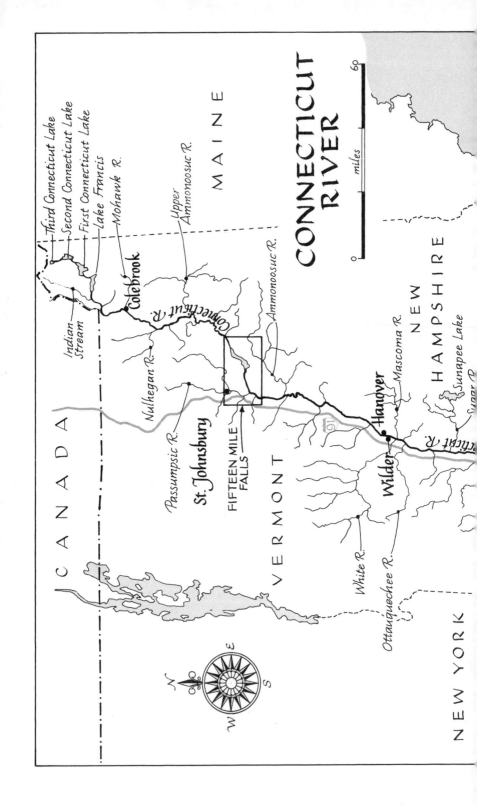

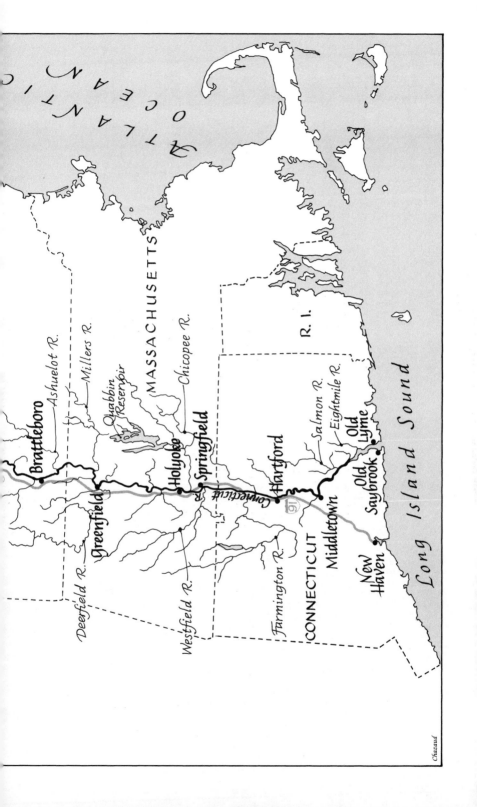

ATLANTIC OCEAN

MASSACHUSETTS

CONNECTICUT

R. I.

Long Island Sound

Brattleboro

Ashuelot R.

Millers R.

Quabbin Reservoir

Chicopee R.

Greenfield

Deerfield R.

Holyoke

Springfield

Westfield R.

Connecticut R.

Farmington R.

Hartford

Salmon R.

Eightmile R.

Old Lyme

Old Saybrook

Middletown

New Haven

91

Chazaud

Foreword

In the summer of 1992, Nat Tripp, myself, and our extended families camped on a sandbar in the upper reaches of the Connecticut River. We had put in at Bloomfield with five canoefuls of children, adolescents, and gear, and lazily floated down the relatively slow, late-July current, passing through just enough Class II riffles to keep the five- to seven-year-olds enthralled. A tradition started that sunny July weekend, and for four or more weekends every summer, even during the week when my schedule permitted, especially if I could mix in official duties, we assembled a flotilla to go down the river. On one trip we fit twenty-six in eleven canoes for a three-day trip, most of it in the rain.

The first time we paddled fifty miles in one weekend, I was still governor of Vermont and was accompanied everywhere by a state trooper. The lucky trooper on this trip, with no previous canoeing experience, dragged my eight-year-old son, Paul, down the last stretch of quiet water above Wilder Dam.

Paul was in the stern. He knew how to J-stroke by then, so he steered, paddling as hard as he could, barely keeping up with the human engine in the front, all the while suspended in the air by his bowman's comparatively huge weight.

Our second fifty-mile weekend finished around Springfield, Massachusetts. The only stretch of the whole river you might not really want to swim in is between Holyoke and Springfield, but of course we swam in it anyway. At the end of a very long weekend, my daughter, Anne, her friend Elysia, Paul, and I climbed into our old Grumman, left all our gear except life jackets and paddles with the cars that were picking everyone else up, and paddled twelve miles in two and a half hours. We had the current behind us, but it was a pretty good pace for one ten-year-old, two twelve-year-olds, and a forty-seven-year-old sternman in his canoeing dotage.

These trips were not all about racing from one place to another. We caught and ate a lot of perch and bass, and a few trout. We met a great assortment of people along the banks, including a lot of folks from Vermont, Massachusetts, and Connecticut who let us camp on their land.

We enjoyed myriad rope swings along the river, and stopped for long fishing lunches, letting the kids explore (and get lost in) the oxbows and swamps that line the river. They felt very independent, and it was a little nerve-racking when they disappeared and wouldn't answer our calls. But they did get to be very good canoeists.

Some days on the big reservoirs north of the New England power dams the kids would complain about how monotonous it was to paddle with no current at our back, and no great blue herons or even bald eagles to distract us. If the wind was right, we'd raft the canoes up and tie them together, three abreast. We'd rig one of the tarps into a giant sail, lashed to the paddles. The kids still had to work — someone had to hold up those paddles — but it was time to socialize, make sandwiches, and eat cookies. And especially time to tell stories. Ghost stories were usually saved for after dark around the nightly fire after the last marshmallow was toasted. (And mine usually ended with a loud yell, which despite its predictability always had the desired effect.)

But during the sailing times, with a stiff wind and a strong chop, Nat, my brother Bill, and I told our kids about out childhood, about past trips. (Bill and I paddled the Allagash in our twenties with our cousins and girlfriends, who, we found out later, spent much of the time plotting to somehow get a helicopter and make an early escape. All managed to survive the eleven days, although the romances ultimately did not.) We told them of camping trips with our fathers; we talked about fishing, and the water, and the dams, and the adventures. We talked about adventures to be.

This is how I got to know Nat Tripp.

Nat had been married to a canoeing friend of mine's sister. By the time that friend and I put together our first river trip, Nat's marriage had long since ended, but he was asked along because he had been running the Connecticut for years. Nat is tall and getting gray. He is married to a wonderful woman, a writer, and on that first trip they brought their mostly college-age blended family with them. Nat is an interesting person, a Vietnam veteran who rarely talks about it, but never seems to resent those like me who did not serve.

Nat knows a lot. He knows a lot about fishing. He knows a lot about canoeing. He knows people all along the Upper Connecticut whom I had only met casually in my official duties. Nat is an environmentalist, but he is a country environmentalist. He knows and coexists with the farmers, loggers, and hunters who make their living in the beautiful land we saw by summer. These people weather the frigid cold that sometimes drops to fifty below during winters that last from Halloween to Tax Day, and "mud season," which turns to summer around the end of May. Spring barely exists in the Northeast Kingdom of Vermont.

Nat wasn't born in Vermont, but his life experience and his willingness to respect others make him a good fit. He is what in the sixties we called "deep"; there is a lot going on under a quiet exterior. A lot of thinking, and as I was to find out, a lot of doing. Nat Tripp is a fighter. He connects things. The trip down the Connecticut wasn't just about fun and spending time with our kids. For Nat it was about the whole world. It was about a world that used to be before Europeans came along and tried to subjugate nature without really understanding the long-term consequences of what they were doing. It was about a whole world of rivers that didn't flow straight to the sea anymore because of huge dams built to keep people comfortable in cities hundreds of miles away. People who would never see what they had done to the rivers Nat knew.

Nat sees the signs of old struggles, remnants of entire villages that disappeared during the twenties to make way for "progress." He connects this to dam-building still going on in Canada and to China, where over a million people are being relocated as the water rises behind Three Gorges Dam. The world is getting smaller, and more and more "progress" means fewer and fewer human beings who have ever run a really wild river. Far fewer who will ever make their living near one.

Nat gets all that. He is comfortable in his own skin, but he is ready to fight. To fight for more rivers and less "progress," to fight against greed without vision, and to fight hardest against those who deny that there is any connection between the incredible rivers and valleys, one of which we spent five years together on, and the healthy future of the world.

Nat knows there is a connection, and he decided to write about it.

Howard Dean

2004

1

This river begins as all rivers do, with a drop of rain, a wisp of fog. It gathers on stone, amid fern, and weeps from the branches of wind-shaped spruce. The movement downhill is silent at first here where the bare bones of the earth meet the sky. The dripping and seeping seems of little consequence amid the tumble of postglacial boulders, the dark silence of high-altitude forest, the lichen, and the reindeer moss. The soil is thin and sour along this rocky spine, which marks the border between New England and Canada. The climate is harsh, and the beauty, stark. To the north, fading through sun-bleached hues of blue and gray, lies the watershed of the St. Lawrence; to the west, the Great Lakes, the industrial heartlands. The river runs south 410 miles to the Atlantic, rugged White Mountains on the left, smoother Greens on the right. On the very clearest of days a brown smudge of hydrocarbon haze marks the distant coastal cities, but the view is often obscured by cloud, which settles down from above or creeps up from below. Everything is dripping and ghostlike in the fog. Summer and winter, storms boil in without warning, bringing ice rime, lightning strikes, powerful winds, more fog.

According to the tradition whereby humans and nature are distinct and separate entities, even adversaries, this is a foreboding place where chaotic nature clearly has the upper hand. In the romantic tradition this is a place to be nearer to God, where one comes to be inspired. Yet all this is an illusion, for even here the hand of humanity moves invisibly with the mist, carrying acids, hydrocarbons, and heavy metals from industries and generating plants a thousand miles and more downwind, and the scars of recent logging run across the slopes like an outbreak of mange. But water works magic, and in a small, serene bowl that the last glacier left amid the stone, the water consolidates to begin its journey. The trip to the sea may take months in a dry time, weeks during wet. It is a course that follows our nation's history, from past to present, gathering our spoor and suffering our politics. Hikers often visit here to witness the beginning, climbing up a steep, narrow trail from the customs station. As always, the water completes the illusion, innocently reflecting the sky.

Nobody has visited through the long winter. For almost five months the snow has drifted deeper. On still, frigid days the only sound was the raven. On still, frigid nights the northern lights made the snow shimmer red and green. Now it is near the vernal equinox, and as the warm sun climbs higher, winter's grip is loosening at last. Chickadees sing their spring song from the spruce trees as the snow slumps lower. Glistening rocks and south-facing slopes emerge from the three- and six- and ten-foot depths of snow. Myriad insects, excited by the heat, scurry from the flakes of bark, the blanket of duff where they have lain dormant for so long. All across this vast, high tumult of ancient rock, the land and the river are reawakening. The water is audible now, trickling through the alder limb dam that beavers have erected at the source. Within the next mile the stream will have dropped five hundred feet in thready cascades, already completing 20 percent of its vertical journey to the sea. It pauses to fill the first of several headwater lakes; pristine, silent, white. There are a dozen named ponds nearby, too, stepping down toward the sea, and maybe a hundred unnamed beaver ponds and bogs lying in the flats between steep hillsides, studded with dead tree stems and stumps that stand out like exclamation points, rimmed with the dark, steeple-shaped spires of spruce and fir.

For ten thousand years this was a hunting ground, sometimes shared and sometimes disputed by the tribes of the adjoining watersheds. Several hundred years ago it was a crossing place for war parties and smugglers. Smuggling still goes on today. Drugs are only a small part of it. Pirated movies and videos, Pakistanis and Guatemalans, computer chips and cattle often find their way through the network of old logging trails, too, although nothing could match the volume of bootleg whiskey in Prohibition days.

A hundred years ago this would have been when the log drives began. All winter teams of men and horses would have been at work, cutting the virgin timber and yarding it to streamside or piling it on lake ice. Then, as the thaw progressed, ten thousand years' accumulation of forest wealth would begin its journey south in forty-foot log lengths in order to build a nation. Driving between fifty and eighty million board feet of lumber downstream each year was rough and dangerous work that is romanticized today, but several lives were usually snuffed out between the rolling logs and icy waters each year, and the only memorial was a pair of spiked boots nailed to the nearest tree. This has always been a place of struggle and bloodshed.

Now the skidders, slashers, log forwarders, and grapples work year-round, and the hills resound to the whoops and moans of high-speed diesel engines. Increasingly, especially on weekends, it is also the song of the snowmobile that drowns out the croaking raven and trumpeting jay as a new recreation economy emerges. The forest resource is declining, and men are being replaced by machines. Ownership of the forests themselves and the mills that processed their product has passed into fewer and more remote hands, gone overseas or gone entirely. Vast clear-cuts, which liquidated the second growth, now sprout brambles and brush, which in turn is supporting a burgeoning moose population, adding to the illusion of wilderness. Tourists come to see the moose. They slowly drive the back roads in air-conditioned comfort, cocooned in steel and safety glass.

There are almost no year-round residents until one reaches the first village, twenty-six miles downstream. It could just as well be a village in Alaska, for here, too, the land has shaped the people as much as the people the land. Skidders, snowmobiles, and log trucks are in the yards alongside swing sets and aboveground pools. In these uppermost towns there is no zoning, partly because it represents government interference, and partly because, up until the recent recreation boom, there has been little measurable growth to be zoned. The frontier lost momentum and stopped here on the farthest fringes of the watershed, and still today the mind-set is often more extractive than cultivative. The plow is still less important than the ax and the gun, and if, as on the frontier, there seems to be an undertone of violence at times, it may be due as much to the harsh and whimsical climate, the hard and dangerous work, as the politics, for in a relationship with the environment that is so often adversarial, individual rights are fundamental; any interference with those rights is deeply resented.

Many of the families in these uppermost headwater inter-vales trace their roots back two centuries to when their ancestors first settled here in the highland crossing between Canada and northern New England. Because of irregularities and lack of clarity about the border, not to mention the smuggling, the settlers here disputed which country they belonged to among themselves until they agreed to form a nation of their own, the Indian Stream Republic, named for the river's uppermost sizable tributary. They had their own constitution, their own laws, and their own army of sorts. The dispute was eventually settled with minimal violence, but the spirit remains inviolate. Land confiscation for storage reservoir construction in the 1930s left lingering resentment, and when the Army Corps of Engineers began eyeing Indian Stream for its next big flood control project in the 1950s, the reception was less than warm.

John works the northernmost farmland of the river valley, where Indian Stream slows to meanders and has set down a fertile plain. There were once a few farms still farther up than his, but they're all underwater now. His is still too far north to raise corn, but he boasts of how well his grass grows here, in the long daylight of summer. He keeps dairy cows and raises sheep, harvests timber, and makes maple syrup in what would have been lake bottom, too, if the government had gotten its way. He points proudly to a newspaper photograph from that time in the 1950s, of his family, holding shotguns pointed south. They are standing beside a sign that to this day proudly proclaims the border of the Indian Stream Republic, even though it is now mostly just a state of mind, but Indian Stream itself still runs free.

John complains that the people here were lied to, that the so-called flood control dams that were built have turned out to mainly serve the industries of recreation and power

5

generation. He fears that the spring floods will return, as they have in so many recent years. "The needs of the little guy who tries to make a living on the land are getting squeezed," he says, with as much grief as anger, speaking not just for himself but for the others around him, too, for along with the fierce independence of spirit there is also a strong sense of family and community, and the well-earned distrust of outsiders is balanced by extraordinary generosity. It pays to listen to his well-chosen words. Like so many of the others up here, he has gained a certain perspective on the rest of us from his farthest end of the valley. In talking to him, I wonder sometimes which of us is worldly, and which the more isolated. Here, the threads of history and generations are still connected to the land. They still are what the rest of us once were as a nation.

Now it is sugaring time, and there is hope for a good sap run. It would help to offset the disastrously low price paid for milk. Soon steam is curling from the woodside sugarhouse. Even the trees are beginning to feel the surge of spring. Here, just above the forty-fifth parallel, halfway between the Tropic of Cancer and the Arctic Circle, the time of snowmelt is thrilling, immobilizing, often cataclysmic. Water gathers in every hillside cleft and starts to wear its way down, an annual passion play reenacting the withdrawal of the glacier ten millennia ago. Frozen waterfalls of ice — turned blue or green or rust red from mineral springs — begin to weep from rock faces, and the frozen earth turns to soup, closing the back roads and skid trails. The waters swirls under ice, rises more and sculpts fantastic shapes. The water is still nearly as cold as the ice itself, and although its purity has already been compromised by ubiquitous air pollution, it is as close to pure as surface water can get these days. You can drink it. It is what gives meaning to the term *headwaters*. These capillaries, these farthest-reaching fingers, are the interface of the river with the sky.

Meanwhile far to the south, where the river meets the sea, the springtime pulse of cold meltwater has kept the broad river swollen for more than a month. It sheens across the mile-wide channel, floating above the salty tide beneath, brushing the greening banks of white oak and silver maple at the feet of lavish estates. Daffodils are blooming. So is the shadbush, punctuating the woodlines with bursts of delicate white blossoms. At the river's mouth, where vast sandbars have long kept big ships out and dashed hopes of a major port, there are schools of fish milling about, bobbing up to sample the exciting tingle of snowmelt, the molecules of Indian Stream, then going back down again to the saline refuge they have known for a year or more. They feel the back-and-forth play of the tides against the shoals, gathering in ever-greater numbers. Some of these fish, such as the shad and other members of the herring family, have always been coming here. Now that the water is cleaner they are coming in greater numbers than in recent memory, beckoned northward along the Atlantic coastline, spawning from the St. Johns River in Florida to the St. John River in New Brunswick, Canada. As their internal chemistry adjusts to the cold fresh water, they begin to move upstream, mostly at night, seeking their natal streams. They have built up extra reserves of fat for the ordeal ahead. They will not even eat until their job is done and the eggs of another generation are in place, far from oceanic predators.

Sturgeons and striped bass will join the upstream rush, too, in what is one of nature's greatest displays of determination and fecundity, but the most revered fish among them all, now milling about at the sandbars, is the Atlantic salmon. One particular salmon, a thirty-seven-inch, nineteen-pound female, has come south, retracing her way down the great North Atlantic gyre from the coast of Greenland. That her conception was attended by a pair of rubber-gloved hands, that her incubation was by stainless-steel trays and electric water pumps, seems of little consequence now. This river once belonged to her kind, too, but they had been excluded from the spawning grounds they preferred farther upstream for nearly two hundred years and hammered by the increasing pollution of the industrial age.

Long after the house lights of Old Lyme and Old Saybrook have gone out, darkening the night sky still farther, and when the traffic on Interstate 95, vaulting high over the river, has dwindled to a minimum, the lights of a few fishermen still bob on the water, driver and striker paired to a boat, one man at the helm while the other carefully pays out the gill nets. They watch the net floats on their two- and four- and six-hundred-foot sets, waiting for that sudden sag, feeling for the thrust against the tide. Aircraft course through the heavens far overhead. The stars slowly turn above the horizon's big-city glow. The fishermen talk while the bankers and brokers sleep. Sometimes a laugh rolls across the water while the changing tide gently hisses against the boats, against pilings and bridge abutments and expensive yachts nestled together by the shore.

Then they haul the long nets in, drenched with cold river water, picking the hard, rainbow-hued shad free of the net, commenting back and forth on the size, sex, and number of them. This is still as it has been here since long before Europeans came, but while there are more fish once again, there are also fewer of these men every year. The small markets are going, and the supermarkets don't care. There are only about a dozen people left hereabouts who know how to bone a shad, which is quite a trick in itself. Besides, there are a lot of easier ways to earn a living. Here, too, as in the headwaters, time may be running out for an occupation that once seemed timeless.

2

Viewed from the distance of the moon, the astonishing
thing about the earth . . . is that it is alive.

— Lewis Thomas

Spring advances northward up through the watershed, covering a hundred miles in a week, rising a hundred feet of eleva-
tion in a day. You can see it spreading: amber, then chartreuse
on the distant hills. Fiddlehead ferns uncurl from the fertile
floodborne riverside soil. Woodland wildflowers hastily
bloom before the leafy shade overtakes them, and birds are
migrating northward along with the fish, keeping pace with
the growing food supply. Now a gentle rain is falling across
the northern hills, which are still gray except for the red blush
of the swamp maples that I've been watching from the house.
I'm listening, too, for as the ground thaws, woods frogs are
the first amphibians to awaken and begin working their way
through the forest to the temporary woodland ponds where
they will lay their eggs, safe from predatory fish. Their croaking is wooden, almost like the raven. Soon they will be joined
by other frogs, spring peepers, toads, and salamanders, and a
more melodically rejoicing chorus of voices will rise above

these vernal ponds, and my pond, too. It means it is time to start the garden.

The rain not only refills seasonal ponds but also recharges the vast watershed of soils and gravel beds and rock fissures deep underground. On average only about half the rain that falls goes into the river — less than that in a dry summer, when the trees act like sponges, and more when the rains come hard and fast or combine with snowmelt. This is what gives the river its pulse: rising in the spring, responding to both the change in seasons and the whims of weather. Plants and animals depend on the river's rhythms to start a new generation. The silver maple, too, casts her spawn upon the rising spring waters, setting another generation in riverbank sand.

I had been fascinated by the flow of water as a child, the way children so often are. I would follow the creeks, build dams and break them again, skip from stone to stone or wade the shallow gravel bars. The water itself was as impetuous as my own life then, and where those streams broadened and deepened, I was equally fascinated by the life they in turn held within. I still am. It is in my blood, so to speak, from the flakes of snow or drops of rain to the sea, and when I came home from Vietnam in 1969, I let the river wash me. It speaks with the voice of a mother, a father, a brother, a lover. It is always changing, it is always the same. I found a place near the river thirty years ago, a little upland valley that would be easy to defend, for I still had the sound of gunfire echoing in my mind. This is the tradition of sanctuaries, of returning to the source.

I was still as young as the brooks that tumbled past, but sharp and on edge. I canoed the river's nearby reservoirs. They were part of the largest hydroelectric complex in New England, still called Fifteen Mile Falls for the cataracts they had inundated, but I kept the dams out of sight, pretended they weren't there, and stayed in the fjords where stone walls ran down the hills and disappeared into the water. As I became a father, this was where my children and I found definition. We camped there as wilderness pioneers, fished there as though it was our only sustenance. I taught each of my children to swim there as they came along. All the while the waters rose and fell to the pull of electrical demand in distant cities. It was a pulse both ominous and, at the time, inexplicable. We began to explore farther, upstream and down, and with time the river smoothed me, just as it has smoothed the stones in its bed.

It was a time of healing for the river itself as well, for of all the images of the preceding tumultuous 1960s, the most important was that perspective offered of the earth by humankind's first footsteps on the moon. The transcendent image of our marbled blue planet rising above the moonscape was created the summer I returned from Vietnam, and for a while everything else seemed less important. That image of our planet, our home, as an organic whole became a symbol of hope at a time of violence and dislocation. The next spring we celebrated the first Earth Day. Within a few more years the National Environmental Policy Act, the Clean Water Act, the Clean Air Act, and the Endangered Species Act were all passed, along with the creation of the Environmental Protection Agency. The 1972 Clean Water Act itself was both elegant and simple, calling for waters to be safe enough for swimming, the fish safe to eat. By the time that decade ended, the change in the Connecticut was dramatic as both industry and municipalities began treating their effluent instead of piping it straight into the river. There was even hope of restoring the Atlantic salmon, and I had visions of salmon in my backyard someday as the effort got under way.

As my children grew more able, we began to canoe the upper river, just below the headwaters, where it runs free for sixty-six miles, running quick through stone in places and meandering lazily through some of the richest farmland in New England in others. I watched the discharge from a riverside paper mill up there change in a few years from a turbid, stinking torrent to a clear trickle. We would count the waterfowl, count the fish we caught, and each year the count went up. If I was naive then, I still am now, still wrestling with my own agrarian dream, still waiting for the salmon, yet all the while I have also borne witness to changes in rural life that are as heart wrenching as war itself. One after another riverside barns have fallen silent; where once the cattle would be basking in the spring sun, heavy with calf, where once the sweet scent of manure would promise another crop, now are found desolation, weeds, sagging roofs, and hip-shot walls.

The surviving farms have gotten bigger, in a grotesque misinterpretation of Darwin: Economics focus on the flow of money into fewer hands, not human ecosystems. For each empty barn, there was a family, a community, a way of life, and now, after a flurry of timber liquidation in the 1980s, the mills are closing, too. This is the same process that is taking place, in varying degrees, all around the world. It is happening in the countryside of Mexico and Central America. It is taking place in rural Asia and Africa. It is happening in the great Amazon basin, the Argentine savanna, the deep soils of the Mississippi Delta, and the coal seams of Appalachia. It is going on wherever the natural resources are rich and people are kept poor.

The river has gotten healthier, but all the while rural America has been dying, and both the culture and the legislation that came out of the 1960s have been subjected to unrelenting ridicule and erosion. We have become so insular, so reactive as a nation that even the conversion to the metric standard, which had seemed a given in the 1970s, has been stopped in the name of a rewritten history of conquest, inch by inch and mile by mile.

The watershed of the Connecticut, like all watersheds, is dendric, leaflike in its shape, with veins running down valleys from the upland margins and converging at the stem. Our civilizations, and our wars against them, have followed this same plan. The Native Americans, who lived alongside the Connecticut for at least ten thousand years, were unified by these watersheds. The river was a means of transportation; the fertile soils and spring runs of salmon and shad were a source of food. The watersheds themselves formed social boundaries. Tribes would gather by the main stem in spring, first to harvest the spawning fish and then to plant their crops. In fall they would disperse up into the tributaries again, each tribe dividing into smaller family groups, each family group spending the winter hunting and trapping in its own upland watershed.

This settlement pattern is common among rivers and hunter-gatherer populations worldwide, but it was already beginning to change when the European settlers first arrived and started following the river's stem northward. Organized agriculture, which was still fairly new to the Native tribes, was making the establishment of larger, more permanent villages possible, with substantial lodges and streets laid out in square grids in certain places along the river's main stem, where the fertile alluvial soils were especially deep and the broad valley created its own mild microclimate, welcoming the south wind. This settlement trend continued to accelerate, frame houses replacing bark lodges, as the new population of predominantly white farmers took over the best lands.

Nearby tributaries powered colonist mills to saw timber and grind grain, and the flow of commerce on the river grew. In time agriculture, too, was displaced and moved upstream during the industrial age while cities, and the wealth they created, became larger and more prosperous downstream. Subsistence farming, hardly more than hunting and gathering itself, still clung to the highest reaches of the watershed through most of the past century, for wealth and population density tend to follow the same pattern as water, gathering and growing as they near the sea.

People in the headwaters today can aptly compare themselves to the brook trout, a native species that once thrived in the entire watershed but has now been exiled to the smallest upland streams where the water is still cold and pure. Brook trout used to grow to the size of a man's arm, or even leg. They were at the top of the piscine food chain, sometimes swimming all the way into the ocean and back, like salmon themselves. More than half of today's resident river fish were never native at all. Bass, pike, and walleye, brown and rainbow trout, and many others were brought here by humans, deliberately or accidentally. These fish, which are more tolerant of warming water, sedimentation, and pollution, have driven brook trout, which really aren't trout at all but a kind of arctic char, into the austere but relatively pristine habitat that also limits their growth. There, these thrillingly beautiful fish thrive in the plunge pools and gravel beds, cool, oxygensaturated water bubbling around them as they forage for insect larvae, nematodes, crustaceans, and smaller fish. It may seem like a stretch to compare this fish to a man in an old pickup truck, wearing wool plaid and an orange hunting cap, but the chances are that he, too, is feeling displaced and under siege these days.

One of the greatest vulnerabilities of the environmental

movement is its elitist reputation. This characterization finds an especially ready ear among the rural American farmers, woodsmen, and mill workers who live close to the outdoors and are already being stressed for economic as well as for social reasons, and their instincts may be right about the Atlantic salmon restoration, which began when a few very wealthy sportsmen got the ear of a few politicians. The salmon has become an icon for both the left and right in an ever-deepening rift. Meanwhile, the Anadromous Fish Conservation Act of 1965 has been quietly and effectively restoring the habitat and population base of less glamorous fish, such as the shad, herring, and sturgeon, with tangible benefits to the river, commercial fishermen, and sportsmen on a budget, but this is not the stuff political speeches and public relations campaigns are made of.

Perhaps the Atlantic salmon restoration is simply the "realpolitik" of environmental marketing. Certainly it is more benign, less Machiavellian than some of the other legislation that has taken shape in lobbies and conference rooms in the past few decades. By the time the Atlantic Salmon Compact was signed in 1983, giving a federal budget to what had been a coordinated state effort on the Connecticut, a parallel systematic dismantling of government regulation was well under way. More foreboding for the river was the growing underground effort to discredit the environmental movement, the 1960s, and that August 1969 vision of our planet entirely. With the appointment of James Watt by the Reagan administration, the nascent "wise use" movement was given a free hand to spread its message of neo-anarchy across rural America, and it did, and still is today. Comprising loosely affiliated resource-based industries, ranching interests, and property rights fanatics, its David-against-Goliath message of the little guy standing up to big government oppression is as seductive as it is misleading. Meanwhile, as stocking efforts have increased almost yearly, the numbers of returning salmon have begun to ominously decline, not only on the Connecticut but also worldwide, and the river's watershed itself has become a battleground.

Part of the nature of rivers is both to unite and divide, forming both a boundary and an avenue of attack. The corridor of the Connecticut has always been strategic from a military point of view, bisecting the heart of New England with its north–south thrust, and nearly connecting the St. Lawrence watershed to the Atlantic coast. During the French and Indian Wars it was repeatedly the scene of bloody massacres, with Indians hired by the Canadian French traveling south to stage raids in Deerfield and other riverfront towns, and avenging colonists such as the Rogers's Rangers going north to inflict similar atrocities. Even now, in the upland hills, there is still here and there a simmering resentment and distrust of French Canadians, although the specific rationale has been forgotten with the passage of nearly three centuries.

These days the threat, sometimes real but mostly imagined, comes from the south, not the north, as the government agencies with their regiments of regulations; as the environmentalists, preservationists, and tourists wend their ways northward, along with the more traditional peddlers. And it is often true that what one person gains to the south, another has lost up north. The best example is the Army Corps of Engineers flood control projects in the valley, which mostly took place during the 1930s and '50s. Upland valley farms were confiscated and flooded in order to protect the investments of power companies and downcountry real estate developers, who had in turn built upon those broad floodplains of Connecticut and Massachusetts, which should have remained as farmland in the first place.

The oppression of local people by big-money dam builders is a part of the rural watershed legend worldwide. The Fifteen Mile Falls hydroelectric project near my home is another perfect example; it was built in the 1930s, inundating fertile farmland, several villages, and the most spectacular cascades on the river, and all the power it generated was exported south to Massachusetts while some villages nearby remained without electricity into the 1960s. While I was growing up in southern New England with television, toasters, refrigerators, and washing machines, the family living in the house I now own was milking cows by hand and using kerosene lamps at night. Even after the Rural Electrification Act was passed during Roosevelt's administration, the utilities continued to drag their feet, running wires in more profitable directions.

Another effort by outsiders was well enough intended, and probably would be of great benefit today had it not met a fate similar to Napoleon's campaign in Russia. In the 1960s Connecticut senator Abraham Ribicoff proposed a Connecticut River national park, saying: "My bill can give to New England what the great western states have long enjoyed . . . breathing space, protected lands, and a place where man can seek refuge from the crowded streets." The purpose was not simply to create a playground for rich city folk. It was proposed also as an alternative to the otherwise intractable poverty and isolation of the Upper Connecticut Valley.

Acceptance of the National Park Service's plan went well downcountry. It was endorsed by New Hampshire's legislators, too, but Vermont senator George Aiken was still furious about the recent dam building and thought the proposal would put the valley's remaining farms out of business. In addition, the plan's representatives had made the fatal error of not courting the favors of local politicians upstream first, before arriving plan in hand. The opposition at public meetings grew steadily more vehement as the team ascended the watershed. More and more ambushes lay in the narrowing valleys. Finally a crowd of almost two hundred showed up at the courthouse in Colebrook, New Hampshire, 363 miles from the sea, on a wintry December night in 1968. Whipped to a frenzy by the rhetoric of local leaders, the crowd sent the plan's proponents limping back downstream and eventually out to sea.

By the time Massachusetts congressman Silvio Conte made a few ambiguous remarks about establishing a "Connecticut River greenway" in a political speech a decade later, and then had the misfortune to die in office before his vision could be defined, the anti-government underground was much better organized thanks to the growing wise use movement. Conte had long been a friend of the Connecticut River and had already seen the establishment of an anadromous fish research center at Turners Falls named for him. He was very popular, dearly missed by many, and it seemed a fitting tribute that his vision of a greenway should be fulfilled. With the passage of the Silvio O. Conte National Fish and Wildlife Refuge Act of 1991, it was the turn of the U.S. Fish and Wildlife Service to mount an assault. The lines of opposition were already in place, put together like Frankenstein's monster, out of pieces of the dead and a few strategic jolts of electricity.

3

The Gods of the hills are not the same Gods as those of the valley . . .

— Ethan Allen

It is an evening a dozen years or so before today. The local zoning board has convened, and I am the freshly appointed chair. Before me is Francis, a gentleman well into his eighties who has been farming the same parcel of land here in Caledonia County that his ancestors settled more than two hundred years ago. This is a very beautiful farm, too, up on the heights and running down to a lake, with an expansive view of more farms and dark woods and stone walls reminiscent of Scotland itself. For all its beauty, it is also a farm that few but he and his frugal, hardworking fellow countrymen could make a living with, but he has. He has also been selling, or leasing — we're not quite certain which — numerous parcels of his lakefront land, and a large number of mobile homes have sprung up on these parcels almost overnight. This is the reason why he is before us tonight, and it is not the first time.

Francis keeps a record of his land transactions, as well as

much of the proceeds, in his commodious overalls. Anytime, anyplace, if, say, one of his tenants questions the terms of a deed, Francis simply feels about and soon produces the proper document. He's not about to share this information with anyone else, though, and besides, tonight he's not wearing his overalls, he's wearing his kilt, and that means that I am in big trouble. This is his fighting garb, and he always wins. But this time, as he rises to smite me, I am as worried about his health as I am my own. He has to push himself up from the chair, and his knobby knees wobble.

He rallies just the same, swings his damning words about the room like a claymore, and holds his ground. I am struck with awe. A few days later, back in civilian clothes, I run into him at the auto parts store. He looks at me, smiles, and says, "So now what will we do?"

Francis is gone, and I miss him now more than ever, still wondering what to do. There never was a more worthy foe. By the time of our last confrontation, I had begun canoeing on the river with the governor of Vermont, Howard Dean. We started doing this when he was just beginning his first elected term, and we kept on doing it off and on until he had gone the river's entire length. Early on, he appointed me to the Connecticut River Joint Commissions, a bi-state advisory body, and one of our immediate tasks was to integrate the proposed Silvio O. Conte National Wildlife Refuge into our River Corridor Management Plan. Each riverfront community had appointed representatives, and our Upper Valley meetings took place on Thursday evenings in that same county courthouse in Colebrook where the national park proposal had met its demise on a cold December night in 1968.

The specific proposals for the refuge had just been released for public comment by the National Fish and Wildlife Service, and they were pretty innocuous, but predictably the plan's reception had been getting cooler as one progressed up through the watershed. Most of the opposition seemed to be coming from the property rights puppets who often attended meetings just to disrupt them, and also seemed to all be reading from the same script. They said that the Conte Refuge proposal meant that nobody would be able to farm or harvest timber within a thousand feet of the river or its tributaries, that in the name of protecting salmon, nobody would be allowed to farm or log at all. It led me to wonder just who was pulling the strings.

The concept of property rights as something sacred arguably had its beginnings in the slave-owning South as a reason why escaped slaves could be fetched back from the North under any and all circumstances. Its revival across rural America seemed like a high-octane blend of conspiracy theories, some of which traced their convoluted path back to the myth of POWs still held by North Vietnam, a brace of Hollywood pulp movies, and various other anti-social militia fantasies. But when I decided to track the story down, my inquiring phone calls led to none other than a representative of the U.S. Chamber of Commerce, that deceptively named self-proclaimed champion of business better known for its newspaper columns and lobbying efforts.

The man on the other end of the line was clandestinely recruiting members in the valley by the coercion of fear. He said secrecy was important, and had the usual "rural legend" stories of local people who were left homeless, jobless, or even dead by government regulations and environmentalists. He wanted to come to my farm to talk more, sell me a membership at two hundred dollars, spread the word like some sort of combination of Mafia shakedown artist and Paul Revere. I began to mumble, sounding anti-social and possibly violent myself. I said I didn't want to talk to anyone and hung up. A brief spell on the Internet revealed a U.S. Chamber of Commerce cloaked in respectability. But a deeper search showed more, and its recruiter was far from alone. Even the John Birch Society had resurfaced (or resubmerged) as a quasi-militia cult against government and environmentalists.

These were not men like Francis, the farmer. These were not men who would stand and fight. These were misfits and cowards who were gaining ground because of the rural malaise. I had heard about the April 1995 Oklahoma City bombing while driving home from a Connecticut River Joint Commissions meeting. The press and public immediately suspected Islamic terrorists, but I felt certain it was one of our own boys from the start. Within a year's time even the bombing itself was rumored by some to be a government conspiracy, along with gun control and supermarket bar codes. When I attended a Connecticut River Atlantic Salmon Commission meeting at the U.S. Fish and Wildlife Service office in Hadley, Massachusetts, a year later, the ubiquitous "Jersey barriers" of reinforced concrete were in place as a bulwark against truck bombs, and the public entranceway had been shunted aside.

The stories that the Conte Refuge was part of a plot for a takeover by the United Nations, the rumors of United Nations blue trucks taking water samples from the river at night, even of blue helicopters and blue tanks lurking in the woods, could have been funny if it wasn't for the threats that were coming along, too. Here and there people who failed to pay their property taxes, who barricaded themselves inside their homes and held off the sheriffs, were being elevated to local-hero status, along with promises of "backup" from quasi-militias of beer-bellied misfits such as Nichols and McVeigh's Michigan Militia, similarly publicized groups in Montana and Idaho, and Vermont's own "UnAmerican

Activities Investigation Committee."

It was only a matter of time before someone really snapped. The weather of that summer of 1997 was tumultuous, too, on edge with long hot spells broken by deluges and dramatic lightning strikes and flash floods that uprooted trees and took out small bridges. Then, at two forty-five in the afternoon of Tuesday, August 19, in the parking lot of the IGA just north of Colebrook, New Hampshire, a man named Carl Drega shot trooper Scott E. Phillips as he prepared to cite Drega for rust holes in his pickup truck. We'd been hearing about Drega at our planning meetings, how he was a ticking time bomb; I'd encountered him on the river, too. He'd illegally filled in his riverfront property, and when I inadvertently landed my canoe there once he ran me off.

To a property rights fanatic such as Drega, automobile registrations and inspections are part of the conspiracy. Phillips knew this about Drega and had called for backup, but he was already mortally wounded when Trooper Leslie Lord pulled up, and Drega shot Lord dead in the seat of the cruiser. The sixty-seven-year-old Drega then coolly finished off Phillips as he was trying to crawl to safety, pulled Lord's body out of his cruiser, put on his trooper hat and bulletproof vest, and drove off in the cruiser to kill the rest of the people who had crossed him in the past.

I certainly would have been on his list had I lived nearby; he had disrupted select board meetings and threatened various officials in Colebrook many times in the past, even shooting over their heads. He had waved his gun at the zoning board of his weekday home in Bow, New Hampshire, when they hadn't allowed him to subdivide his property there. Yet after so many armed confrontations, the only legal action against him had been a court order prohibiting him from carrying a gun into public buildings. Now he carried an AR-15 assault rifle even when he walked out to his mailbox, and there were rumors, which proved to be true, of bombs and booby traps all over his property.

Of all the people Drega hated and had threatened the most, an attorney named Vicki Bunnell was at the top of his list. She had been the chair of the select board when he first threatened to kill her for insisting on a property appraisal he thought was too high. She had taken this and subsequent threats seriously enough to occasionally carry a gun in her purse. Everybody liked her, knew how terrified of him she was, and when he showed up at her office, which she shared with the local newspaper, just down the street from the courthouse, she and the others inside fled in alarm, screaming warnings to others.

Drega shot her in the back seven times, killing her instantly. An editor from the paper, Dennis Joos, managed to tackle Drega from behind and hold him for a moment, but Drega was incredibly strong, a rigger by profession, and he broke free and mortally wounded Joos. He then got back into the cruiser, its windows shattered by gunfire, drove down the street a short distance, and parked in front of the courthouse, which also houses the local police. He waited for any police to come out. None did, so he drove to the home of a former selectman and kicked down the front door, but he wasn't home. He then drove back to his own home, rearmed, and set the house on fire to destroy any evidence.

Back in the cruiser and listening to the calls of alarm and confusion on the radio, he drove across the river to Vermont and set up his ambush on a railroad bridge just north of the confluence of the Connecticut with the Nulhegan. He now had a laser sight on his assault rifle, a nine-millimeter pistol, a bulletproof vest, and hundreds of rounds of ammunition. Deputy Game Warden Wayne Saunders was responding to

the radio calls when one .223 round from Drega came smashing through the windshield and hit his badge before entering
his chest, sending him crashing into a tree. Assuming
Saunders was dead, Drega got back into the cruiser and
drove a few more miles down the Vermont shore, turned into
a narrow dirt lane in the woods, and set up another ambush
by a sacred Abenaki spring. (Saunders lived.)

Perhaps Drega chose this place to make his last stand
because it is the most sacred known Native American site in
the Upper Valley and is said to carry a curse of its own. More
likely he was just looking for a deserted lane to duck into.
Drega waited a long time while cruisers zipped back and
forth on the road. Then a local constable and his son, who
happened to live just a few houses down, decided to check
the lane. Moving in silently on foot, they heard the cruiser's
radio and then spotted it abandoned in the woods. They
called for backup. Fortunately, among the many responding
law officers was a Vermont State Police German shepherd
named Major, who detected Drega's hiding place behind a
huge tree uphill from the cruiser.

Drega opened fire, but at a greater distance than he had
planned, and what followed was painfully familiar to me, the
kind of long summer evening I, too, have known, with dark-
ness gathering in a deeply forested place, and shots cracking,
and men calling out. The police had nothing to match Drega's
firepower, just shotguns and handguns, and Drega wounded
three more of them before a pellet of buckshot entered his
mouth above the vest, broke his jaw, and exited through the
back of his neck. He was knocked unconscious and quickly
bled to death. Four more handgun rounds were found
embedded in his vest.

I recount this in some detail partly because of my own
pain, which goes beyond unpleasant memories of Vietnam

and a lesson in politics gone wrong. It is more than that, more than a matter of murder and betrayal and the seeds of dissent deliberately sown in unstable minds. Here, on an August afternoon, was the bloody unraveling of America. And the worst part was that within days, when the community was so grief stricken, having just lost four beloved and outstanding citizens, militia and property rights groups across the country started publicly proclaiming Drega a hero.

Just before the killings, our local St. Johnsbury, Vermont, paper — one that has, for three generations, been the conservative voice of the North Country — had given Drega a degree of approbation by stating in an editorial that it was understandable why some people would want to take the law into their own hands when faced with present-day government regulations. It was the sort of thing one heard, and continues to hear, in the shops and on the streets; there are lots of rural legends about people being jailed for filling in mud puddles. But for a while the Drega killings caused the local militants to fall silent. People began to think twice before going public with their inflammatory rhetoric.

Our planning meetings in the Colebrook courthouse became somber, overshadowed by the drapes of black crepe and photographs of Drega's victims on the wall. Those four people — two state troopers, an attorney, and a newspaper editor — were beloved pillars of the community, and were killed precisely because of what they were and what they represented. Their pictures hang there still, and still elicit grief. The Conte Refuge, which in the end was mostly a matter of cost shares and conservation easements to protect critical habitats, was gradually accepted.

4

Piscem natare doces.
(You're teaching the fish to swim.)
— Anonymous

The watershed of the Nulhegan, at 151 square miles, is only seventeenth in size of the greater Connecticut's thirty-seven watersheds, but of them it is by far the most pristine and, in terms of ecological values, the most important. Lying in the northeast corner of Vermont's Northeast Kingdom, it is unsullied even by villages, almost entirely unpopulated besides seasonal hunting and fishing camps. The Nulhegan, its waters stained a tea-like color by the tanins of sphagnum bogs, cedar swamps, and spruce-fir hillsides, rises up, hand-like, through the fingers of the East Branch, the Black Branch, the Yellow Branch, and the North Branch to touch watersheds flowing north. It is a place where vast, flat bogs are broken abruptly by rugged hillsides, where fast water alternates with slow, dark, log-choked meanders and blue beaver ponds. Although it has been logged extensively for well over a century it managed, until recently, to hide those scars well and is still home to many rare boreal species such as the spruce grouse and the Canada jay. The native brook trout thrives in the waters of the Nulhegan and is said to be especially colorful there, with gemlike reds and yellows and greens and blues.

I was drawn to the Nulhegan basin as a young man and spent many days exploring on the logging roads or by canoe. I remember once encountering an old man with a six-pack of beer perched on the roof of his truck, and a six-shooter in his hand, who was whiling away a weekend afternoon drinking beer and shooting at the empty cans all by himself. Our visit began with my asking for directions; I was looking for South America Pond, just one of the many isolated ponds in the uplands that, in those days, could only be reached on foot. When he learned of my quest, he wanted to talk more of his own days there, the things he had seen and done, and he got tears in his eyes when he said how he wished he was young again, too, and seeing this place for the first time.

I returned a few years later as a fledgling journalist, accompanying state biologists and professional hunters in a quest for black bears. We were running the bears with dogs, tracking the dogs with radio collars, and darting the bears with tranquilizer guns after they had been treed. These were midsummer days that began long before sunrise, and were well under way with the dogs baying in hot pursuit of a bear by the time the sky grew gradually lighter, and the spires of spruce and fir emerged from the mist, and the rugged peaks would brood against pink curtains of sky. The bears would lead us to places we never would have seen otherwise. Trying to lose us, they would find islands of old growth that loggers never could reach, and we would climb over moss-covered hulks of fallen giants. The bears didn't like the bogs any more than we did but they loved to swim, and we would swim after them through the cool tea-colored waters.

The Nulhegan basin was singled out above all other habitats for its intrinsic values by the Conte Refuge plan, and when the Champion International paper company offered it for sale, it became the only major federal land aquisition in the Connecticut River watershed. Its confluence with the Connecticut is also the place where Carl Drega made his stand, and where I stood on a chilly day early in May, waiting for a hatchery truck to show up with one hundred thousand freshly hatched Atlantic salmon fry. The tree Saunders had crashed into after being shot was just a hundred feet away, still showing its wound after several years. With me were a couple of Vermont fisheries biologists, some student volunteers from Dartmouth College, and a bunch of high school students with Ken, their science teacher, from Colebrook. I've known Ken for years through our planning meetings; in summer he has a fishing guide business on the river, and he's a dedicated advocate of the river's health as well as a respected teacher. He often gets his students involved in river issues such as restoring eroding banks, and the stocking of Atlantic salmon fry here was a new opportunity to show them both ecological values and how science might be able to improve them, *might* being a key word I was confident Ken would discuss later.

The technology of raising fish by artificial means in hatcheries and using them to stock waters is not especially new, dating back well into the nineteenth century, a time when humans were discovering all sorts of new ways to industrialize nature to their needs. Once it was discovered that fish were almost as easy to breed and raise as corn and chickens, hatcheries in Europe and the United States went to work, mainly using the fish they raised to please sportsmen. The biggest problems are keeping a steady supply of clean, fresh water and preventing disease. The longer a fish is kept in a hatchery, the more difficult it is to keep it healthy, so they are generally set out in the wild as soon as they are big enough to assure a reasonable rate of survival.

Salmon were stocked in the Connecticut as early as 1869, with thirty thousand placed in Vermont's West River. A million were stocked in 1874. Despite the lack of adequate upstream and downstream passage at the many dams, some excellent returns of sea-run fish were reported, with a much better success ratio than today, but there was no regulation of harvest, fish could be slaughtered as they lingered at the foot of impassable dams, and industrial pollution was on the increase. Hatchery programs subsequently turned their attention elsewhere: to inland streams and lakes where the harvest could be better controlled, and to the Pacific Northwest, where the interests of both dam builders and salmon canners could be served at once.

Unable to resist the temptation to play God here in New England, hatcheries introduced many non-native species that were easier to raise, such as western rainbow trout and European browns. These introductions quickly dominated most New England trout waters, a notable exception being the Nulhegan. To this day most New England inland fisheries are managed on a "put and take" basis — that is, the state puts and the fishermen take at a regulated rate, as on supermarket shelves. The idea of a "natural" fishery, where the emphasis is on improving the habitat of native species, is only grudgingly gaining acceptance.

There is still some debate over just how important the Atlantic salmon ever was in the Connecticut River. Stories of salmon runs so huge that it was a crime to feed salmon more than three times a week, or that people could walk across the river on the backs of fish, are the apocryphal inventions of writers and real estate promoters. Analysis of bones and scales in the midden piles of the Native Americans on the river are ambiguous, as are colonial records. Runs of fifty to a hundred thousand fish were likely, which is still a lot of fish but far less than the shad runs of today. The shad was always a far more important food fish on the Connecticut, too, but nothing can match the adulation for the Atlantic salmon, *Salmo salar*, "the leaper." It has been prized for its flesh and admired for its acrobatic determination throughout its historic range, which runs in an arc from northern Spain, up through Scandinavia, and across the North Atlantic to perhaps as far south as the Hudson River.

A sense of this fish's special status can be attained simply from the names that have been given it during its different life stages. Starting as eggs in a *redd* or nest, then *fry* like other fish as it hatches in the gravelly beds of clean, quick-running upland streams, it is next known as *parr*. The parr will remain near the place of their birth for from one to three and occasionally four years, attaining a size of six or seven inches and requiring both habitat and diet similar to trout. Then one year, as the daylight lengthens and the water warms, the dark patches on the parr's sides begin to fade, and they start to journey downstream. They are now known as *smolt*. The behavioral and exterior changes are accompanied by interior hormonal changes as well, adapting them to the salinity that would have killed them as parr.

Once in the ocean, New England salmon travel up the coasts of Newfoundland and Labrador, feeding on vast schools of capelin and krill, and joining the other schools of salmon from European shores to fatten in the rich waters off Greenland. If they return to their native streams the next year on their first spawning run, they are called *grilse*. They are called *kelt* after they have spawned. They are not technically *salmon* until they return after two years or more at sea. There is little doubt that they once spawned in the Connecticut's Nulhegan and considerably beyond, vaulting the natural barriers of Turners Falls, Bellows Falls, and Fifteen Mile Falls. They are known to be able to leap as high as twelve feet, fighting their way upstream against the high spring flows. And unlike their western salmon cousins, Atlantic salmon do not necessarily die after spawning. They can return again and again, attaining legendary size.

Nobody knows for certain how salmon find their way back to their natal streams, and — contrary to the common story — not all do. A certain percentage of them will try new rivers; otherwise they would not have returned so quickly after the glacier melted. But most probably follow the unique chemical traces of minerals and organics in the water back to the place of proven success, just as scientists are able to take a small bone called an otolith from the heads of anadramous fish and analyze the trace chemicals in it to determine which rivers that fish swam in. Rivers, and their tributaries, each have their own "fingerprints" that can be followed to the source, and are recorded in layers of fish bone.

The natural fishery for the Atlantic salmon was long gone from the Connecticut River when the movement to restore these fish to the river was revived during the late 1960s, led by sportsmen who customarily spent thousands of dollars traveling to Labrador, Norway, Scotland, and Ireland to catch salmon. They recruited supporters to their cause with extravagant salmon dinners and more fishing trips, and one of the first legislative results was to restrict the harvests of commercial fishermen. The promise of the Clean Water Act and the growing environmental movement added momentum. There was money to be found in the pockets of wealthy

environmentalists to counter the well-funded business interests, and the salmon issue had marketable appeal. After a hia-
tus of nearly a century, the stocking of Atlantic salmon
resumed on the Connecticut. In the years since the Atlantic
salmon restoration first began in the late 1970s, the public
outreach has become increasingly important — and it's a
good thing, too, because the restoration itself has not been
going all that well.

The year 1981 is still the best for numbers of returning
sea-run salmon on the Connecticut. Five hundred twenty-
nine were counted, while the stocking levels a few years earlier were about a quarter million fish. Now stocking levels
are exceeding six million, while returns are getting progres-
sively lower, hovering around two hundred, then one hundred, and most lately less than fifty. Nobody has a good
reason why this is taking place to varying degrees throughout
the Atlantic salmon's range. Blame is generally pointed
toward the ocean: predatory fish or seals, or overfishing.
Meanwhile the public investment here has grown enor-
mously, not only with the program itself, but also through
industry as more dams and their operations are mandated to
modify both design and operations to allow fish to pass up
and downstream. The restoration effort itself has driven a
wedge between the environmental community and business
interests. The vision of the earth gained in 1969, a vision that
included all of us, is fading farther from view.

Our river commission had been hearing an increasing
number of complaints about the salmon restoration program
from the public, especially in the upper watershed. Fishermen
complained that hatchery-raised salmon were displacing
native species such as brook trout in a replay of the management errors of a century ago. They wondered about the expense, the low return rate, and just who would ever benefit.

Management discussions had long ago shifted from how much to charge for a salmon fishing license to how to protect them even more. What if salmon were declared an endangered species and nobody was allowed to farm or log within a thousand feet of a tributary?

There was also some dissent within the ranks of fisheries biologists themselves. A prominent suggestion was that efforts should be focused on a few selected tributaries of the Connecticut first, instead of the whole watershed, with an emphasis on habitat restoration and incremental measurements of success. In 1996 our commission held a public meeting with the salmon restoration experts and presented them with the many questions that had been raised about the program. As expected, they were on the defensive when it came to both investment and prospects. The last public accounting available was only up to 1988. A hundred eleven million dollars had been spent by then: forty-four million by the USFWS, ten from the states, and fifty-five million from industries, mostly in dam and operations changes. A million came from other sources such as advocacy groups. Surely the investment had more than doubled since then. But success was harder yet to measure, the scientists explained. They were trying to develop a new genetic strain, and salmon were an important indicator of the river's overall health. Many other species were benefiting, they claimed.

In most ways our meeting was a wash. We were looking for good science as well as economics but didn't press too hard; we still had to live with these people. The one clear message that seemed to get through to the Fish and Wildlife Service was that it had to do a better job at public relations. Otherwise little would change, and little has. Be that as it may, participating in the program does give citizens some working experience with the watershed, its dynamics, and some, if not all, of the problems encountered, and that's a good thing, as they say. Student projects are under way in classrooms across New England using curriculum packages furnished by the Atlantic Salmon Commission, and volunteer groups are recruited to help with water-quality testing and population sampling, as well as stocking.

On the Nulhegan the morning of our stocking project, a Vermont fisheries biologist began by assembling the volunteers beside the hatchery truck and talking about the restoration program — how salmon had once spawned in these waters, and could again. He repeated the claim that salmon always return to the river of their birth and went on to explain the problems of pollution and dams, how they were being overcome, and the life cycles of salmon and their habitat needs. We then formed a convoy of vehicles and began to follow the hatchery truck up along the highway heading west, beside the Nulhegan's main stem. Every few tenths of a mile the truck would stop; one volunteer would go forward to get a white plastic five-gallon bucket and about a thousand tiny fish. Because I knew the territory, Ken asked me to go along with April, one of the Colebrook students. After we got the fish, our mission was to walk downstream, stopping every ten feet or so to put twenty or twenty-five fish in the water. But this was not the same Nulhegan basin I remembered from twenty years ago. This part had been brutally logged the year before, probably during a wet time of year, just before the Conte Refuge took over. In order to reach the water we had to climb over and under fallen timber, navigate piles of limbs and treetops known as slash, and wade skidder ruts carved three feet deep into the fragile soil. It was a no-man's-land of shattered tree bones more reminiscent of warfare than harvest. It even smelled bad, of festering tree wounds and earthy entrails.

Waders aren't the best thing to wear when climbing through slash. April had borrowed her father's, and she was afraid the sharp splinters would put a hole in them. We passed the bucket back and forth, our baby salmon sloshing about, on some sort of slapstick spawning run ourselves. When we finally reached the water we were at the top of a sheer twenty-foot cliff, with the river, swollen with snowmelt, surging against the rock wall. We circled around, finally made it down to a safe spot, let some fresh river water sip into the bucket to adjust the temperature, and then dribbled about two dozen fish out. With April safely under way, I went back out to the road to my truck and drove downstream to a bridge where the East Branch of the Nulhegan entered.

I walked through a meadow overgrown with alder toward the river. This seemed to be a recently abandoned farm field. Flood debris was lodged about shoulder high in the bushes, along with abandoned appliances and cans in an old junk pile, the usual signs of agricultural distress. At last I reached the water, rushing through a field of small, round boulders, parted by a small island of spruce. The river was making its own gravelly sound as it rushed toward the sea. There was a sense of timelessness, stones steadily being rounded, the river wearing down. There were bits of brick and broken glass in the water at my feet, already smoothed and rounded, too, not by tumbling but by the constant brushing of water and sand.

April was working her way toward me, still playing mother fish. But what about the fish that were already there? Would they get along? Logic dictates that since salmon and trout share both similar habitat and similar diet, something had to give; the river only had so much room, and the laws of nature dictate that the room was already taken.

This was the first stocking of Atlantic salmon in the Nulhegan watershed, and it was billed as a "habitat suitability" study designed to assess the potential capacity of the Nulhegan for salmon. In the fall volunteers and biologists would return with electroshock equipment and nets. They would stun the fish, dip them out, count them and assess their health, then put them back to recover. But some were saying this "study" was a devious ploy, an attempt to forward the agenda of dam removal by using existing federal laws protecting migratory species.

And the future was indeed grim for any survivors of our bucket brigade, should they become smolt and head toward the sea. If perchance they were not eaten by brook trout or the notoriously predatory rainbow and brown trout farther downstream, they would next encounter Fifteen Mile Falls, not yet a third of their way to the sea. Fifteen Mile Falls, which is today not a falls at all but a complex of hydroelectric dams, is the largest such facility in New England. If they made it through the spinning turbines or over the top of the first dam in Gilman, Vermont, they would enter the vast, still waters of the uppermost and largest reservoir. Without a current to furnish clues, they might just stay there. Or they could plunge 180 feet through the turbines or over the top of the next one, to another, where more still water and another almost 200-foot plunge awaited them. Seven more dams would still lie ahead before they reached the sea.

And at almost that same moment, the thirty-seven-inch female salmon that had been lingering by the shoals at the river's mouth was beginning her journey upstream. She was probably incubated at the White River National Fish Hatchery in Bethel, Vermont. She was headed toward a tributary of the West River near Brattleboro, Vermont, where she had been stocked as an unfed fry in the spring four or five years before, just as we were stocking unfed fry on this day. There, in the shallow upland riffles, she had survived the predation of other fish, otters, and pisciverous birds. Most that were stocked with her had not. When her time came, she had endured the downstream passage through the sluiceways and turbines of four hydroelectric dams, running a gauntlet of still more predators: main stem bass and pike and walleyes, then estuarine striped bass and harbor seals. Once in the ocean, her complex hormonal programs ran successfully; she was not desiccated by the salinity. She joined others of her kind in the great wheeling migration. She escaped the commercial fishermen who followed the schools with sonar and satellites along the northern arc of the Atlantic journey.

Her survival to this point is sufficient miracle in itself, and her value, as the carrier of a new generation unique to the river, can probably be calculated in the hundreds of thousands, if not millions if the investments by private industry and utilities are added to taxpayer money. But the hazards yet awaiting her go far beyond those instream or at sea. They extend to the halls of legislatures, the boardrooms and banks of America as well, and our own future as a species would ride with her, too, as she retraced the path to her origins. She had become a symbol for both sides in an escalating and increasingly violent battle, a symbol of success, a symbol of purity, a symbol of guile.

5

The result, therefore, of this physical inquiry is, that we find no vestige of a beginning — no prospect of an end.
— James Hutton

A natural, unregulated river carries more than just water and fish. It also carries the land, and it was this great insight by the English physician James Hutton at the close of the eighteenth century that led to the birth of modern geological science. He realized, while watching a river flow, that he was also witnessing a great geological process; that as hills and mountains were worn away there must be an opposite and equal process, one even greater than the obvious volcanoes, causing mountains to rise and explaining the presence of fossilized clams in the Alps.

On the average, but with wide variation, a flow of one cubic foot of water per second carries twenty pounds of sediment per day. Most of the time this is a gradual process. In a time of flood, the sediment load increases dramatically. A doublingof flow can increase the sediment load eightfold. These fluctuations in flow and sediment load are what make rivers dynamic. What may even seem cataclysmic to humans in our brief lifetime is but the slow beating of the river's heart. The river gives, and the river takes away. In times of flood, the beds of gravel and bars of sand are cleansed and renewed. Plunge holes and scour holes that have gradually silted in are reexcavated. Fine soils and silts are lifted up into the floodplain, renewing fertility; bars of gravel and sand are built up. The vertical profile of the river's bed is restored, and the slow march of mountains into the sea continues, tipping the scales of plate tectonics.

Most of the time this is a constant process. But upland streams can increase their flow a hundredfold during flash floods. Sometimes all the beaver dams in a watershed will go at once, adding to the dramatic rush that takes trees, roads, and houses along for the ride. When one stands beside a flood like this, the earth trembles. Boulders the size of automobiles boom audibly as they tumble downstream. Automobiles themselves quickly disintegrate, reduced to an engine block and widely scattered bits of scrap metal within a few miles. Days later, the narrow valleys emerge transformed. Hillsides are denuded, having slipped away, and broad alluvial fans of sand and gravel spread across the valley floors. This contributes to the sense of revolution, of violent change, that the headwaters convey.

Downstream, the big river reacts more slowly. A tenfold increase in flow is a big one, and broad floodplains absorb the impact, allowing the waters to spread out, slow down, and settle out the heavy sediment load. But even after the flood recedes, the dynamics of sediment transport continue, upstream and down. Remove sediment, either by mining it to build roads or by building a dam, which acts as a sediment trap, and the sediment-starved river will devour its banks elsewhere. The slowly moving mass of sediment in the river's bed provides a degree of stability; without it the river begins "head cutting," carving a deeper channel in the material upstream in order to fill the void below. Occasionally bridges have suddenly tumbled into rivers far above gravel extraction operations when their abutments became unstable, the gravel beneath them having eroded away.

No matter how large or small, where the valley broadens and the water slows, it begins to meander in a series of graceful curves, for rivers, too, feel the Coriolis effect of the earth's spin, and their flow, too, spins like a corkscrew as it travels downstream. Given a uniform bed, the river's course becomes a sine wave, with the wavelength and amplitude depending on flow and gradient. Erosion and deposition of sediments is a constant process at each bend; centrifugal force throws water against the outside bank, cutting away at it, while fine sands and silt are deposited on the inside bank.

It is in the sixty-six miles of unregulated river above Fifteen Mile Falls that fluvial geomorphology best works its magic. Here, in the last truly rural and least spoiled reach of the river, the Connecticut writhes like a serpent through some of the richest farmland in New England, with a broad sandy beach and a deep fishing hole every half a mile or so. There is plenty of firewood at the high-water mark, where the beach gives way to silver maple forest, and sweet ostrich fern grows six feet tall in the rich soil and deep shade of the trees. This is where my boys and I still like to make camp for the night, going off barefoot in the deep clean sand, teamed up to gather wood, fish, or pitch tents before dark.

I have canoed this particular stretch of river at least once every year for almost thirty years. I also return for one day each spring for what is called the Essex County Conservation District Field Day. It is one of my favorite spring rituals, and here I am once again in this broad valley, where the river meanders through rich farmland. I am outside the cow barn just about half a mile south of one of our favorite places to camp. We're on a low hill with the flat valley floor spreading out below us. It is nine in the morning; the herd of Jerseys have been milked and are ambling out to pasture. Newly born calves are basking in the sunshine outside their igloo-like plastic calf shelters, and the morning's barn chores are just about done. I can hear the clank of pails and the murmur of voices in the milk room, and the smell of manure blends with that of disinfectant soap.

A bunch of us gather here each May to give the local fourth- and fifth-grade schoolchildren a taste of farm life and a sense of what conservation means. Most of us work for the government as foresters, soil scientists, or agronomists — the proud but beleaguered remnants of a rural tradition of public service that dates back to the founding of the land grant colleges in the mid–nineteenth century. But there aren't many government license plates on the cars pulling into the barnyard now; anti-government rhetoric has become so fevered that most use civilian plates now. Besides, each year, each rural agency suffers more cuts in staff and funding. There isn't much room left for government information with so many corporate salesmen around. There are just eleven farms left in the whole county anyway, and the few county agents remaining are busy distributing information on coping with depression, along with agriculture.

I'm one of several "civilian" volunteers, and I feel privileged to be here this morning, in the twilight of a way of life. Faded jeans, plaid shirts, and caps advertising fertilizers, equipment, or herbicides are the uniform of the day. Some of us gathering here know each other well. We sit on boards or commissions together. We've helped draw up management plans, gone to innumerable public hearings, endured the slings and arrows of the neoanarchists, and wrestled with the doubts and reservations that are so much a part of the rural character. Others here I only see on this one day each year, but there is still a sense of comradeship. In a way, for me, it is like being in the army again, in the best sense of what the army was. We share a vision, an idealism that is all but gone today. I'm from the government and I'm here to help you.

As always, the leading conversation is about the weather, and now it is dry. The hired man is already out in the field below us with the disc harrows getting it ready for corn, and a long tan plume of dust is trailing him around the field. I can see another plume of dust rising above the line of silver maples where the river is; they're getting ready to plant corn on the next farm, too, while there is still enough moisture left in the soil to germinate the seed. I've been here on mid-May days when it was spitting snow, or when the fields were still puddled with spring floods. This year the spring came hot and dry. The apples are blooming and the shadbush is just about gone by, and there are constellations of yellow dandelions blooming in the bright green meadows below.

The buses arrive, six of them, and the kids come piling off, accompanied by their teachers and special aides. Everyone is fascinated by the calves, and there are few things more endearing on earth than a fawnlike Jersey calf. The kids jump back gleefully as the calves lick their outstretched fingers. They didn't expect the tongues to feel so rough! Then they are all gathered together for introductions. First, the farm family that is hosting us is introduced. They stand there, proud and a little self-conscious, too. This year the son is running the place, his father has had some health problems, but things are running well. The son and his fiancée are just in their early twenties, but it turns out she's a whiz at milking and that can make all the difference. A good milker, someone who has a natural way with cows, can be what makes a farm succeed and is getting harder and harder to find.

Then it is time for us to go down to our stations. As usual, mine is down by the riverbank, almost half a mile away. I go down the same path the kids will take, down a wooded path past the forestry station. The woods are vibrant with emerging leaves. Steve, the county forester, is putting cards on various trees, listing the uses for each species. He's listed some price comparisons, too: 75¢ for a pulp log, $1.79 for a two-by-four, 50¢ for a candy bar. "Sixteen species within a short walk," he boasts to me.

I continue past him, out onto the open floodplain where an old cutoff oxbow of the river has formed a small pond. Will, a wildlife biologist, has his green pickup down there, and he's laying out a collection of animal pelts and plaster casts of tracks. He'll talk about wildlife habitat, and I'm a little on edge talking to him because at the moment I've got a snowshoe hare living in my kitchen and that's against the law here in Vermont. I'm not sure whether he knows about this or not.

Then I'm alone, following the long sinuous thread of the cow path out across the meadow. There is a flock of Canada geese gleaning the stubble of last year's corn in the next field over. A raven croaks as it flies overhead. Beyond the line of silver maples the stark peaks of the Percys and Cape Horn rise, still some snow in the highest points. It seems more like a scene from out west than New England, it is so broad and open, with flat fields at the foot of steep mountains.

I reach the river. Bloodroot is blooming in the shade of the maples. I can see the first group of kids moving out of the woodline toward me.

I can tell what kind of a class I'm in for by the way they move across the field. Some are orderly, ducking under the electric fence when they have to, and staying on the path. But some come across like a herd of wild animals, breaking away, balking, going astray, and by the time they get to me I've lost some valuable minutes. When I see a class like that coming toward me I start going toward them, too, so I can meet them halfway. I work hard to get their attention. I wave my arms at the mountains and jump up and down talking about the glacier and the forces of erosion that shaped this valley, but there are constant interruptions and I begin to despair. These are kids from the school districts where the property tax base has been pulled out from under, where the unfunded mandate of "special education" is draining everybody's energy, where ADHD and the drugs to treat it have found a market niche, and both teachers and parents are just too tired to fight it.

Other groups are wonderful, attentive and under control, and I can get worked up into my frenzied presentation without distractions. As we approach the river itself, I ask them to look at the tree line ahead of us. I tell them that the trees here are maybe fifty or sixty feet tall, but that once this field was filled with white pines that were often more than two hundred feet tall. The Native Americans called this place the *coos*, pronounced *cohass*, meaning "place of white pines." I ask them to imagine what it was like here back then, in the twilight of the great forest. I ask them to look around and see how the land here is not really flat at all, see how it undulates. This is different from the more uniform flatness of the floodplain farther down the river. Here each low rise, each depression, represents a place where the river once meandered. But those trees were much taller than the river is wide; as the trees tumbled in, they jammed up and formed dams, making the river meander even more.

I enjoy imagining what this looked like myself. It was, on a huge scale, what one sees only in isolated upland streams today: a complex of trees that often rivaled giant redwoods in size, shading the river where they stood, some leaning, others fallen and forming huge barriers with root masses the size of houses, roaring white waterfalls plunging over the logs, followed by pools dug thirty feet deep into clean gravel beds. Mud and silt were relegated to the old, stagnant cutoff channels, crescent-shaped oxbow ponds, and fetid swamps.

I also enjoy imagining the travails of Rogers's Rangers as the band of cutthroats found themselves entangled here, trying to find their way back to Massachusetts after having slaughtered the women and children of a St. Francis Indian village late in the autumn of 1759. The warriors picked them off one by one as they climbed over logs and waded swamps. Starvation took others until there was just a handful left, still carrying the loot, which consisted mainly of a silver triptych and chalices given the Indians by the French missionaries who had converted them. I spare my young audience these details, but do add that it is no wonder this was the last part of the valley to be cleared, long after the hillsides had been put to agriculture.

Hopefully, we have reached the river by this point. I ask them how many like to fish. Almost all the hands go up. I ask them if they like to catch brook trout in the small streams. They respond enthusiastically. Then I tell them about the giant brook trout that used to live here, and how they were the biggest, strongest fish in the river. I tell them about the salmon, too, and how they used to come up this part of the river, and might again, too, but I catch myself; I'm not going to market this fish like a drug salesman would, or a fertilizer salesman. There are some mighty big dams between the ocean and us, and a lot of other issues, too.

I turn to the subject of agriculture, and ask how many of them live on a farm. Sometimes no hands go up, and sometimes I get a few. A generation ago most hands would have been in the air, and I'm astonished at how little many know about farming even though it surrounds them. I tell them that all great civilizations began beside rivers because of the rich soils, how wealth begins with soil. I show them how we are trying to stabilize the river with streamside plantings to prevent the erosion of valuable soil — but I often lose them at this point, and especially this year, because the spring floods have deposited a refrigerator on the sandbar in front of us, and that is the one thing everyone seems really interested in. Toward the end I give in and just try to address the refrigerator questions.

Then it is time for them to move on to the next station, where Tim and Jean from the Soil Conservation Service have filled trays with dirt and sod and set them at various slopes. They'll pour water on the trays and talk about the mechanics of soil erosion and remediation. At noon we all gather for lunch at the cow barn; everyone brings their own sandwich, but there is lots of free milk. None of us would think of bringing a soda; the milk is as much a part of this communion as anything else, and it has never tasted better. "I want them to hear about the good stuff," Steve says to me as we walk back down to our stations. "It sometimes seems like they only hear about the bad stuff."

The good stuff. Years ago, when I was between marriages and I used to canoe through here with my two very young boys each summer, we used to spend a second night on a sandbar farther downstream where some local kids the same age or a little older would spend the entire summer building a kingdom in the sand. They built it near where we camped, where the coarser sand began to mix with silt and was the perfect consistency for making "dribble" sand castles, an esoteric and Dr. Seuss–like style with lumpy spires and minarets and crenellations. Castles and great walls and highways and guard towers would spread along the riverbank for a hundred feet or more until some freshet would wash it away, and then they would start all over again. By the time we got there in August those four or five local boys would be tanned to a dark brown — mine would be, too — and they'd all stand in a circle and compare their GI Joe action figures and invite my boys into their games.

There was one boy who was a little older, obviously the leader and the arbitrator when there were disputes over property or procedures in the kingdom. I often ended up talking to him while the others returned to their game. I admired his work a lot, admired the way he handled himself and his responsibilities, and at one point I said I thought it was a wonderful way to spend the summer. "But there's nothing *else* to do," he complained, and I immediately understood. Idyllic as it may seem to be in the sand and water every day, there is another world beckoning, roaring, in fact, from the television, in the malls, in the schools, and in his blood now. "Market forces" have taken over, and the kingdom is doomed. I believe he was twelve that year, and it was the last year that I saw him.

I started thinking about that refrigerator again on my drive home. Somebody probably dumped it onto the frozen river as some sort of protest. There has been a lot of this going on since the municipal landfills started charging fees. When the ice broke up, the refrigerator got carried to my spot, an in-your-face statement of rural malaise. Mandatory recycling, too, was being sabotaged locally, with people deliberately contaminating materials, for of all the things that the family farm represented, hard work and impoverishment included, the most important one was independence. It is the loss of the traditional independence, more than anything else, that gives rise to the anger. And if you think it isn't important, just remember that most of the high school shootings, along with the Timothy McVeighs and Ruby Ridges, have been distinctly and disproportionately rural. Springfield, Oregon. Notus, Idaho. Littleton, Colorado. Jonesboro, Arkansas. Paducah, Kentucky. Pearl, Mississippi. Fayetteville, Kentucky. Edinboro, Pennsylvania. This isn't the inner-city minorities the press likes to rail about. This is the heartland of white America, all stirred up by greedy hands.

For an outsider, a flatlander, a person who has been removed from the travails of rural life by half a dozen generations, the rural character is likely to be the object of derision, of jokes. Since the coming of the industrial age, the stereotype of hicks, rednecks, and trailer trash has come to be applied with increasing frequency. The media, and television especially, will make rural life seem romantic while selling margarine made in factories, but for the most part in today's largely rootless and suburban society it seems to require a degree of ignorance, if not insanity, for rural people to work so hard for so little material gain. Farming often appears to mean little more than endless hours of grueling work, in the cold rain or hot sun, broken only by the unpredictable opportunity to be crushed, delimbed, or impaled by one's own equipment. The fact that so many still want to do it shows it must mean much more.

On my drive south toward my home there is one last riverside farm I pass before the highway begins to twist and climb to the hills that make Fifteen Mile Falls. This last and biggest of the Upper Valley farms looks almost like a southern plantation, the way the three-story brick federal farmhouse sits at the end of a long drive surrounded by vast, flat fields. I've spent a lot of time with Chester, the man who farms it. We walk his fields — which lie between river meanders, ringed by distant mountains — looking at alfalfa and talking. He can trace his family roots in farming all the way back to the *Mayflower*, farming in Massachusetts, then southern

Vermont, and now here, moving up the valley like an Indian himself, he says, but there is more to it than that because he's smart, too, improving his investment along the way.

He's a wiry, bearded man with the name of his farm proudly embroidered on his work shirt; he named it for the color of his wife's hair, and now his two sons work the farm with him. He's a lot less comfortable talking than he is farming, but when he talks about farming it is with deep, religious-sounding conviction. Still, like other successful farmers, he likes to boast. He boasts of corn that is fourteen feet tall, boasts of four and even five cuttings of alfalfa, for farmers, the best of them, are also some of the most competitive people I have ever met. He's always ready for a lively debate, too; right now he's got a running argument with one of his sons over the merits of no-till over conventional plowing. The salesmen who are always coming around don't stand much of a chance with him, either. I don't think he's ever bought a new piece of equipment. He and his sons talk things over and go around and pick things up used at the auctions, and they spend much of the winter in their shop, welding, inventing, and improvising.

As the timber industry began to collapse, farmers found it harder to get sawdust to use as bedding for their cows. Cows are healthier and milk better with plenty of good dry bedding every day, so this farmer got an industrial shredder and began to pick up the bundles of old newspapers at the nearby recycling center, shred them, and put them in the stables. He quickly found out that people were sabotaging the newspaper bundles with nails and bits of barbed wire; it was the anti-eco equivalent of spiking trees to thwart loggers, and with a similar effect. Just as a spike would ruin a saw and possibly injure the sawyer, a spiked bundle of newspapers would hit the shredder and send sparks and bits of molten metal flying about. So the farmer and his son took to examining each bundle with the same magnetometer that airport security guards use, but they missed a bit of wire one day and the sparks set the pile of shredded papers on fire, just when the south wind was blowing strongly up the valley. Within minutes the cow barn was blazing. Now, a dumb thing about cattle is that they don't understand fire at all, and will run into a burning barn to hide, but the son thought fast and used his tractor to smash the walls of the barn down, driving the cows out. They lost about six cows right away, and six more were badly burned by the time the fire was put out, but they saved most of the herd and the milkhouse and were milking again that evening. It is, in fact, the elemental struggle itself that delivers its own reward, and this, too, is increasingly incomprehensible in the vast land that lies beyond the divide of Fifteen Mile Falls.

6

The only sure bulwark of continuing liberty is a government strong enough to protect the interests of the people, and a people strong enough and well enough informed to maintain its sovereign control over its government.

— Franklin Delano Roosevelt

Government is like a big baby — an alimentary canal with a big appetite at one end and no responsibility at the other.

— Ronald Reagan

Land shapes the water and water shapes the land in a constant back-and-forth play; streams slip over rocks on their way to the sea, wearing away a few millimeters of stone each year in their silken way, more where the rock is soft, less where it is hard, focused by gravity, moving toward the center, gathering strength. Within the average watersheds of New England, it is generally said that one square mile generates one cubic foot of flowing water per second. The Nulhegan, for example, with a watershed of 151 square miles, can be expected to contribute the equivalent of a bumper-to-bumper parade of VW Beetles going past at about seven miles per hour, or a freight train crawling at less than walking speed. With every successive mile in the river's main stem length, a few more cubic feet of flow are gained, and the influence on the land is stronger. With each pour over ledge, with each quick run through fields of boulders, the river's voice is lower, louder, deeper. By the time the river reaches Fifteen Mile Falls, where a vein of especially hard rock and a fault line cross diagonally, a flow of sixteen hundred cubic feet per second slips past on average, about the same volume as two freight trains, side by side, traveling at five miles per hour.

A cubic foot of water weighs about sixty-four pounds, the weight of a small anvil, and it has considerable force when dropped from a height. Nobody knows exactly when early civilizations first put this force to work, but there are ruins of Roman water-powered mills, and drawings from China dating back two thousand years. The emperor Justinian had mills in mind when his code of laws was drawn up; the concept of riparian rights made rivers public property, with the rights for their consumptive use being doled out by the government as long as those uses served the greater public good — a term that has been stretched in every direction imaginable ever since.

In both Roman times and the first centuries of this nation it was mostly the smaller mountain streams that provided power. There was no reinforced concrete. Dams were small and often temporary, expendable structures built of log cribs, boulders, and planks. As settlement spread up the Connecticut Valley, a mill to saw the wood and grind the grain was usually the first commercial structure, and it would run seasonally depending on the water levels and work at hand. There were often dozens of mills in watersheds that are now almost entirely deserted. Only a few stone abutments still stand in the woods where the biggest mills were; evidence of the more common smaller ones has all been swept away.

Placing a dam in the main stem of the Connecticut was a costly and dangerous undertaking that began with the industrial age. In the nineteenth century huge textile and manufacturing mills began to grow beside the river downstream, with paper mills favoring the upstream locations, closer to their source of pulpwood. The International Paper Company was the biggest of those in New England, and it bought the water rights to most of the best mill sites on the upper river. When the generation of electrical power began to look like an even more profitable enterprise, International Paper created the New England Power Company and transferred the water rights at the best sites to it. New England Power in turn began building dams, big dams, first on the Upper Deerfield River tributary in southern Vermont, and then on the Connecticut River main stem at Vernon and Bellows Falls, slowly working its way upstream toward Fifteen Mile Falls, which was the most promising and challenging site of all. In each case the government granted it the right to do this, sacrificing the rights of private property in favor of the public good, as it had since the time of Justinian.

When the construction of Comerford Dam was begun in 1928 at the foot of a long cascade known as Mulliken's Pitch, the bodies of four river men were discovered buried on the bank, stuffed inside pork barrels. This pitch was the most hazardous part of the spring log drives going south, just as it had marked the traditional end of navigable waters for travelers going upstream. Those simple graves spoke volumes about both the power of the river and the sacrifice of men; there were many more people lost here whose graves were never found. Such was the way of life here, violent and occasionally heroic, and while it could be argued that these men,

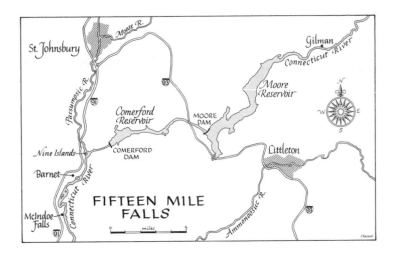

and their deaths, helped to build a nation, it must also be said that they helped to build a fortune for a few timber barons who never got their feet wet.

Three dams were proposed for the Fifteen Mile Falls complex; Comerford would be the first, the tallest, and the most difficult. There was local opposition. There always is, and it is almost always overwhelmed. In this case the promise of both jobs and a huge boost in tax income for the affected towns silenced all but a bitter few. Hydropower was promoted as "white coal," a northern Appalachian alternative to the drudgery of subsistence farming. The river valley here was narrow, isolated, and impoverished. The falls themselves had always been seen as more of a liability than asset, a barrier to commerce. The land nearby and upstream remained underdeveloped but for a few small villages, and bypassed by major thoroughfares.

With the promise of prosperity, strong public schools, paved roads, and streetlights for the local communities that would remain above the proposed high-water mark, lines were surveyed, claims settled, forests cut, buildings razed, and cemeteries relocated. A railroad spur was constructed, vaulting over the Passumpsic River on a curved steel bridge just above the Nine Islands confluence and then running up alongside the Connecticut for a few more miles to the dam site. A concrete mixing plant was built beside the tracks. Stone and sand were quarried locally, and material was moved by rail to the top of the dam site by a series of switchbacks. Barracks and other facilities including a movie theater were constructed for the thousands of workers, who were largely Italian immigrants rather than local. Steam-powered shovels and dredges did most of the heavy lifting, but the most commonly used tools were the shovel and the wheelbarrow.

Comerford Dam, named for the man who was president of New England Power at the time, now rises above what was once Mulliken's Pitch as a 210-foot-tall concrete monument to that era. Transformers and service buildings add another forty feet to the dam's height. The scoured rock bed of the pitch lies at the dam's foot. Although bereft of water, it's easy to see how salmon once climbed up it, from ledge to pool in successive steps. Now this bony remnant of the river is dwarfed by the dam itself, towering above. Huge twenty-foot-wide concrete buttresses on the nearly vertical dam face are connected by shallow arches and bracketed by what appear to be siege towers. It is a bold architectural statement as well as a dam, complete with flourishes cast in iron on railings and lampposts that speak of that exuberant era just before the Great Depression. Dams like this will never be built again, and now the concrete is spalling, weeping lime and water, adding to the monstrous Gothic presence of the dam that straddles the neck of the valley. The railroad line remains in place, trees rising between the ties.

The powerhouse sits at the dam's foot, accessed by elevator above a canyonlike tailrace that was carved through the rock of the pitch. The AC hum coming from within is audible half a mile away. It sounds like a huge hornet's nest. Inside the powerhouse's classic Palladian windows, in a space that resembles Grand Central Station, four 54,000-horsepower generators are fed by tubular penstocks sixteen feet in diameter. A gantry crane traverses the powerhouse eighty feet overhead. Human attendants, watching gauges, lubricating bearings, are dwarfed by their creation. Side doors lead elsewhere inside the dam to machine shops, cafeterias, and offices.

Comerford Dam was designed to operate as a peak generating facility. By the 1920s it was clear that electrical loads would vary widely through the day, and while electricity cannot practically be stored until needed, water can be. The narrow but deep six-mile-long reservoir behind the dam would be allowed to fill during the night, serving as a massive storage battery when electrical demand is low. During the day, mainly in the morning and then again in the evening, one, two, or occasionally all four penstocks would be opened to meet the rising demand of cities far to the south. The river's bed below the dam, which had been dry, is suddenly flooded. "White gold" pours forth with a roar.

President Hoover, whose name would soon go on the nation's next big dam project, began the dam's operation by pushing a symbolic red button in the White House. By then a second, smaller dam had been built five miles downstream at McIndoe Falls. Although it, too, would generate power, its primary purpose was to even out the pulses of water flowing from upstream. This was out of concern not so much for the riverine environment as for the six more hydroelectric dams that lay still farther downstream. Construction of the third dam in the Fifteen Mile Falls complex was postponed until the 1950s due to low electrical demand. Now Moore Dam rises at the upstream end of Comerford Reservoir, spanning a broader valley with its art deco concrete head works and extensive earth fill, with a broad lake reaching eleven miles behind it amid steep, wooded hillsides. All that remains of the original Fifteen Mile Falls is a short reach at Nine Islands, where the Passumpsic and the Connecticut join, between the tailrace of Comerford and the headwaters of McIndoe, isolated and untouched but for the periodic flushing of peak power demand.

As the largest hydro project in New England, the dams at Fifteen Mile Falls are also a unique monument to the stubborn New England character, which prefers private money to public. Even larger projects followed, all across the nation, in the Tennessee Valley, on the Colorado, the Columbia, and elsewhere, but only in New England were the advances of the government so stubbornly resisted. It was deemed more honorable to pay higher electric rates, and even to sit in the dark as so many communities did in the decades that followed, than to invite the hand of big government. During the Second World War and afterward, the accelerating flight of industry and development to the south and west was due as much to the warm reception of Washington down there as to the warmer climate.

In the valley of the Upper Connecticut, resistance to the National Park Service in the 1960s and the U.S. Fish and Wildlife Service's Conte Wildlife Refuge in the 1980s were simply the continuation of a long tradition, while the region's economy continued to decline. Government regulations made farmers store their milk in cleaner and refrigerated stainless-steel tanks, instead of sending it to market in traditional cans. More small farmers went out of business. Resentment festered while the milk processors and distributors consolidated, grew bigger, prospered, and strengthened their grip on the market. Manufacturing jobs continued to dry up, moving first to the Sun Belt and then overseas. Forlorn hill farms were bought by outsiders like myself. Downtown storefronts remained vacant.

I was having troubles of my own in the 1970s; some of us got a farmer's market started, which still thrives today, but the novelty of growing for it wore out fast. Our farm was coming back to life, though, with adventures in various types of livestock subsidized by outside income, and those cerulean reservoirs of Fifteen Mile Falls were right next door, always inviting an afternoon picnic, paddle, or fishing trip. If I had been more attuned for it, I could have seen the changes coming back then in the 1970s. For example, almost overnight the housing complex I was accustomed to driving past near Comerford Dam simply disappeared. Comerford Circle had been a little village, almost, of attractive '30s-style homes built to accommodate the dam workers and their families. Then it was gone with no trace but the driveways. Even the cellar holes were filled. The days of corporate patrimony were over, and anyway worker housing rang of socialism.

I should have seen it coming again a few years later, when I was canoeing and fishing on Comerford Reservoir with my then very young sons. A huge power transmission line had just been constructed, running down across the hills in a tonsured strip through the forests from a vast new hydroelectric development in northern Quebec to the Comerford substation, following almost exactly the same path as the raiding parties of both sides during the French and Indian Wars. I paid little attention to the Cree Indians who showed up in

Vermont to protest, on a public relations warpath against the flooding of their land. And I paid little attention to the explosions that resonated off the hills surrounding our fishing spot on a clear summer morning. I thought it was a farmer blowing stumps with dynamite, and still didn't make a connection when we paddled around to the next cove and saw a small brushfire burning on the shore, with nobody anywhere nearby.

We landed, and being civic minded got out and began stomping the flames out and bailing water on them, until I found what appeared to be the source of the fire, a sizable fir tree that seemed to have been struck by lightning, bark shattered and peeled. I puzzled over that, on such a fine day, then looked higher and saw the transmission line looming above us, cables as thick as ship's hawsers. We had barely fled back to the canoe and gone offshore when there was another explosion and lightning arc from the line back to the tree again. A white mushroom cloud blossomed upward, and the blaze resumed. I called the state police. I called the power company and received a reprimand. The explanation took a lot more digging. This was an experimental extra-high-voltage DC line, and they were testing it that day by cranking up the voltage and seeing what would happen. The point was that this was big power, driven by big politics, I was to find out later, and one had best not get in the way.

The 1970s and early '80s had been hard on utilities. Nuclear energy, which had promised to deliver power "too cheap to meter," was in fact turning out to be both expensive and dangerous. After the Three Mile Island near meltdown and the cancellation of the Seabrook, New Hampshire, plant, environmentalists were increasingly blamed. Then came the energy crisis, which was bad enough itself, but the conservation measures that followed almost killed some utilities.

Consumption wasn't growing as fast as predicted; there was a surplus of generating capacity. When electric utility executives saw the telephone business deregulated in the early 1980s, it got them thinking, always a dangerous thing.

The Public Utilities Regulatory Policy Act (PURPA) of 1978 had been perceived by them as yet one more abomination. It required utilities to purchase power from renewable resources. But upon closer examination by legal teams, it seemed the legislation that had been intended to conserve energy and develop alternative and renewable resources could in fact be turned into a fatal chink in the regulatory armor. According to PURPA, if someone in Vermont wanted to sell "green" electricity generated by cow farts, he had to be allowed to send it out to anyone in the national power grid and get paid the going rate. A little old lady in Pasadena could buy it. They wouldn't be the same electrons, of course. She'd just be tapping into another corner of the vast interconnected reservoir of electricity. But if that was so, the utility lawyers argued, then why couldn't a factory in the East buy dirty but cheap power from a coal-burning plant in the West?

When Ronald Reagan took office in 1982, the deregulatory breeze became a tornado, as did the effort to discredit almost everything associated with the 1960s: the anti-war movement, hippies, and environmentalism. One of Reagan's first acts was to remove the solar panels that President Carter had installed on the White House roof. His administration wanted to put the memory of the energy crisis behind as quickly as possible. It had been almost as humiliating as Vietnam itself, and image was becoming everything. Solar panels are for losers, just like small, energy-efficient automobiles. Private foundations and "think tanks" began to multiply, divide, and reorganize around the Beltway like plankton in the warm sunshine, reshaping public images and privately unraveling government. Some, such as Citizens for a Sound Economy, were deliberately disguised and produced studies showing how consumers would benefit by deregulation, while privately gloating over the potential windfall for investors. It was the beginning of a grand and opulent masquerade ball that continues to this day, and by 1992 Congress had enacted legislation allowing utilities to join in the rush toward deregulation, leaving the details to be ironed out by individual states. "The Greens are going to have to eat this one" crowed a *Forbes* editorial.

All this still seemed far away while we paddled the waters of the Connecticut in the mid-1990s. Moore Reservoir was particularly impressive, with thirty-three miles of undeveloped shoreline. It was, and still is, an aesthetic gem of New England despite water-level fluctuations that rival the Bay of Fundy. When I canoed it with Governor Dean he quickly recognized how special it was and resolved that we should act quickly to ensure that the shorelands and eight thousand acres of adjacent unbroken forest should be protected. He was not the first politician to feel this way. Moore Reservoir and the lands around it would have been a keystone to the National Park Service proposal, and the state of New Hampshire had investigated including it as a part of the White Mountain preserve.

This time, though, a lower-key effort involving conservation easements might work. The Federal Power Act of 1986 had determined that environmental considerations, such as migratory fish passage, had to be included in all new licenses for hydroelectric facilities, and the Federal Energy Regulatory Commission license for Fifteen Mile Falls was due to expire in July 2001. Negotiations for the terms of a new license presented an opportunity to assure both the conservation of the shoreland and modifications of the dam operations so that they would be less harmful to water quality and habitat.

I joined the negotiating team representing our bi-state river commission. There were also local, state, and federal agency representatives, as well as other "interested parties" such as regional and national environmental advocacy groups. It made for an interesting blend of lawyers, scientists, and bureaucrats, and many millions were at stake.

All dams have effects on rivers that go beyond the most obvious one. Nutrients and sediments are impounded along with the water, settling toward the bottom. The still water stratifies, warming on top and remaining cold on the bottom, and biological activity in the nutrient-rich sediments uses up available oxygen at lower depths. The composition and distribution of all species living in the water changes dramatically as a result, and of course migratory fish are blocked entirely. There are changes in the river downstream as well. Often dams discharge from penstocks deep under the surface of the reservoir, so that water reentering the river is both colder and lower in oxygen. It is also sediment starved and more prone to erode downstream riverbanks.

As a peak generating facility, however, Fifteen Mile Falls was having an even more profound effect on the various habitats in the reservoirs and downstream. The fluctuations in level on the reservoirs themselves made it difficult for many species of shallow-spawning fish to reproduce or shoreline and aquatic vegetation to survive at all. In the river below, times of a nearly dry riverbed alternated with flash floods several times a day, and the natural cycles of the season were almost entirely gone. But power generated to meet peak demands is also a lot more valuable — often three or four times as profitable as power generated by "run-of-the-river" operations. Compromise was going to be difficult, but we began in good faith by touring the dams, the reservoirs, and the adjacent shorelines. Potential habitats were mapped, above the water on foot and in boats, and below the surface with sonar. We intended to come back and have every important habitat explored in detail, from the babbling feeder streams to the stygian depths. We asked for, and received, both flash floods and droughts downstream at Nine Islands, where the last fragment of river remained. We paid no attention whatsoever to events still farther downstream, under the jurisdiction of Massachusetts.

Meanwhile in Massachussets, the home of New England Power, the legislature was among the first to respond to Congress's new permissiveness. The move toward deregulation there began with a corporation which was a major employer and user of electricity that had already worn out its welcome in the legislature by coercing tax credits year after year with threats to move away. When it changed its tune to a plea for energy deregulation, the legislators were relieved. Other business groups and lobbies quickly piled on. With the promise of lower rates for everyone, the legislature moved. Utilities such as New England Power were ordered to decide whether they wanted to be an unregulated producer of power or a regulated transmitter. New England Power decided to become a "wire" company — that is, it would transmit rather than generate electricity. It preferred to remain a regulated utility, as it always had been. The hydroelectric facilities at Fifteen Mile Falls, and the public trust that went with them, would be auctioned off to the highest bidder.

7

. . . Nature never did betray the heart that loved her.
— William Wordsworth

My fondest memories of school are the times when I was supposed to be in it but wasn't. I could find more in the swamp down below the high school than I ever could in the classrooms. Before I got thrown out of college, I spent a lot of time down below the campus where the Fishkill River enters the Hudson in a quiet cove. One evening the herring were spawning, and a remnant band of Catskill Indians were catching them in dip nets. Later they showed me how they caught snapping turtles by feeling about for them in the river muck with their bare feet. I liked being an outsider, remaining one even as an officer in the army, which inevitably drafted me. Watching the sun set over the Mekong gave trust, as natural things do in a war, and I remember that with the moments of sunset with my family on the shore of the Connecticut, or the porch of our farmhouse.

I have tried, at certain miserable times, to join the crowd. I remember a morning in May when I was in Parsippany, New

Jersey, working for AT&T with the prospects of a permanent position. I went for a lunch-hour walk outside our drab industrial building, one among many like it, and came to a field of dandelions blooming; in the distance beyond a line of trees wearing the first frizz of green was a dilapidated barn about to succumb to the bulldozers. I was on the next plane home. I've become wary of men wearing suits, having tried one on myself, but it is a lot harder at times for me to articulate my own inner direction than it seems to be for them to articulate theirs.

They have "a fiduciary obligation to their shareholders" that seems today a holy order of evangelical absolutism, against which "outsiders" form frail bulwarks of science, social need, and law — and the law especially is getting shakier all the time. Our ship of state is beset by teredo worms, and we could hear them gnawing as we negotiated the settlement agreement for Fifteen Mile Falls.

Our negotiating team had been stunned at the politics in Massachusetts, a state that had not been represented at the table and that we really hadn't been paying attention to. It was quickly agreed that it would be better for us to come to terms with a known entity. What if the new owners wanted to develop the shoreland property, install a giant waterslide, and make the whole thing into a theme park? What if one of the industry's notorious "bad players" won control, a company with a stable of ruthless lawyers and renowned disregard for regulation? There were already some ominous names circulating: Hydro-Quebec, Pacific Gas and Electric, and a newcomer called Enron.

It would clearly benefit New England Power to present a settled license agreement along with the sale terms, instead of the likelihood of prolonged litigation and no guarantee of outcome. Yet we had barely completed our reconnaissance.

The next step would have been for several years of detailed studies to be performed, with long periods of yawning interrupted by occasional fistfights. All parties decided it would be best to come to terms quickly, without the benefit of studies. We were encouraged by the additional promise of a conservation easement on all the company's extensive landholdings if we could come to terms, and most of the scientists had a pretty good idea of what the studies would reveal anyway; only the details were absent.

The executives doing the negotiations for New England Power had been as blindsided by developments as we were. The company had generally earned a good reputation environmentally over the years, and the tone of our early negotiations had been much more collaborative than confrontational. Cleve, who headed the team for the utility, was about the same age I was, had spent time on the boards of various environmental organizations, and was a fellow river commissioner as well. We spent many pleasant days together on the waters of the reservoirs or in the bowels of the dams talking not only about the issues before us but also about our families and other things we had in common. He reminded me of some of the senior officers I had known in the military, very respectable with a broad smile and a quick wit. Even though we were on different sides, we became and remain friends.

It was a friendship that would be sorely tried, for almost a year of constant brawling followed. The company wanted to preserve the value of the complex by maintaining its ability for peak power generation. We wanted to determine what that value was in order to negotiate. The company wanted to inflate the value, on the one hand, because Merrill Lynch was putting the works up for auction, and simultaneously deflate it because it was renegotiating their tax assessment with the various riverside towns. Lower taxes would be an inducement to prospective buyers, too.

Cleve was, above all, the voice of the corporation, and like a good officer he would not waver from his mission. There were times when we were absolutely furious with each other, much as adversarial lawyers might be, when we were doing our jobs at the negotiating table. When we met outside we were still friends, but it was never easy. Some advocates wanted to eliminate the peak generating entirely; others wanted to keep the water lower in the reservoirs to restore portions of the original river. But that would mean higher property taxes for nearby residents. What is the value of a warm-water species, like bass, compared to a cold-water species like trout? And how can the value of river flow be compared to electricity anyway?

Cleve seemed to be under more pressure than the rest of us; deregulation had forced him into more of an adversarial role than I suspect he was comfortable with. Profitability and contempt for regulation, for sentimentality, had to be countered by solid social or biological science or, in certain cases, the law, which would prevail in the case of the Atlantic salmon restoration. Fish ladders, which are really stairways of connected pools, were in place at dams downstream, but there was no way they would work here, with ascents of two hundred feet or so. The proposed solution was for mature sea-run salmon to be trapped below the dams and trucked around the complex. It was something they were doing out on the West Coast, but there they were working with salmon stocks that were already well established, and despite a lot of sanguine claims it wasn't working well. An alternative proposal put forth was to use funds instead to restore salmon habitat on tributaries such as the Passumpsic, which entered the Connecticut just downstream of the dams. It was a proposal based on better science, and it focused on habitat instead of confrontation, but the restoration advocates had the federal law as well as their own dogma on their sides and wouldn't back down.

In June '97 we were sequestered for three days at the governor's mansion in New Hampshire. Time was running out. We would fight in the conference room under the glazed eyes of a huge stuffed moose, then retreat to our respective caucuses. It was very tense until somebody started playing the Darth Vader theme from *Star Wars* on a nearby piano whenever Cleve entered the room. We came close to a deal, did two more days at a motel, and in the end reached an agreement that was a national landmark and a tribute to the value of collaboration over litigation. The stakeholders agreed that they had an interest in the value of the facilities. The company agreed that the operations did have impacts, and they would pay a certain amount into a mitigation fund. Payments to the fund would increase with the profitability of the facilities. The money would be used to restore habitat on tributaries such as the Passumpsic, while the company could continue peak generating operations with some limitations. Reservoir drawdowns were limited during bass spawning in spring, and a minimum flow through Comerford Dam was guaranteed, so that the river would not be dewatered. It was a settlement worth about fifty million dollars in terms of operational changes and expenses; the fund would get between twelve and sixteen million, depending on the profits of the project.

A major reason for allowing the dams to continue peak power generation was to protect their property tax value to the local towns. Other values, such as habitat for frogs and turtles, were written off. They'd continue to be killed off each winter by water-level drawdowns. There isn't much "value" associated with frogs and turtles. Salmon passage, both upstream and down, would be implemented according to the outcome of various studies to be performed by the dam owners, and among the studies was one called *Atlantic Salmon Smolt Migration Through the Moore and Comerford Reservoirs.*

And so it was that a few years later I was standing outside the powerhouse of Moore Dam on yet another beautiful morning in May. Ten thousand cubic feet of water were coursing though the penstocks beneath my feet every second, a freight train going a mile a minute, while the steep surrounding hills were aglow with spring. Moore Dam, constructed in the 1950s, doesn't have the embellishments of Comerford. The Great Depression had a sobering effect on utilities, and this dam was all cool concrete efficiency except for an art deco visitor center on the New Hampshire shore and expanses of vast, closely mowed lawn around the maintenance buildings and transformers.

I had to strain to hear what P. J., the dam's maintenance supervisor, was trying to tell me. I lost some hearing in Vietnam and it was almost impossible to discern his words above the roar of water and whine of turbines. He was telling me about his fish. He had been put in charge of a tank full of salmon; about a hundred of them, six or seven inches long, were in a round fiberglass hatchery tank outside the generating room, endlessly swimming in a circle. The dam itself towered a hundred feet above us. A white, hissing, foaming swirl of tailrace water poured from the dam seventy feet below us, then slowed to curls and boils, and finally melded into the vast blue pond of Comerford Reservoir, the next one down, resembling, for a moment, the river that all this once was.

This caring for fish was quite a novelty for a man who had

spent most of his working life lubricating and repairing the enormous machinery inside this dam and the two more downstream. A local person and a fisherman, if he had an opinion about the plan to restore the Atlantic salmon to its historic range above the dams he was discreet enough to keep it from me. He was pleased that only three of the fish had died since they'd come under his care a few weeks before, keeping the water clean and fresh and feeding them handfuls of pelletized fish chow. If this was an affront to his own good sense, it was only the latest of several lately. When he started with the company he was one of about two hundred workers. By this time there was just a skeleton crew of a dozen keeping the dams running, and in a few more weeks there would be nobody at all on nights and weekends. The whole complex process of flow regulation and power generation was being automated. Alarms, sensors, and other security devices were being installed. The bronze bushings and oil pressure pumps that he had spent half his life ministering to were being replaced with Teflon. It may save money now, he conjectured, but it could only lead to trouble later.

I was there to witness the smolt migration study called for in the license settlement. Only the smolt under P. J.'s care weren't smoltifying on schedule. All across the Northern Hemisphere, from Kamchatka and Siberia to Scandinavia, from the Canadian Maritimes to the Pacific Northwest, the white birches were dangling golden chains of flower and the two- and three-year-old wild salmon parr were undergoing profound physiological changes. Their coloration was changing from dull, mottled olive on the sides to silver, and the black patches were fading away. The shape of their heads was changing. Their body chemistry, the balance of hormones and electrolytes, was changing. This was happening everywhere but here, it seemed, in this one fiberglass tank.

The mission was to see if these young salmon would be able to navigate the broad, still waters of Moore Reservoir and figure out which end led to the ocean. There was considerable debate in scientific circles as to whether they could manage this without any current to guide them. Then, if they reached the dam, there was a question as to whether they would be knowledgeable enough to dive down forty feet to the penstock opening; and if they managed that, what would happen next? Tailrace fisheries are among the best in the world, because that's where the big predatory fish hang out, waiting for those other stunned and battered fish that had the misfortune to pass through the turbines. Would we just be adding salmon to the menu?

Our more immediate problem was that these hundred fish seemed out of step with the rest of the world. For two weeks they had just kept on swimming in circles in their fiberglass tank, as they had since hatching two years before, trapped in their own incredibly bland universe. Finally Brian and Tim, two biologists from a consulting firm, showed up, both bearded and outdoorsy looking. They dipped a few fish out of the tank, examined them, and grimaced with disapproval. Perhaps the water temperature wasn't high enough. Perhaps the tank itself wasn't getting enough sunshine. At any rate, they would have to be in the maintenance supervisor's hands a bit longer. But they hadn't driven all this way for nothing. We were going to spend the rest of the day looking for six salmon that had seemed to be smoltifying when they were released into the headwaters of the reservoir three days previously.

Our search for six small fish in a body of water eleven miles long covering thirty-five hundred acres was going to be made easier by the radio transmitters that had been inserted into them. Just as the business of environmental consulting has blossomed in the past decade, largely as a result of court decisions, so has the technology and the resultant field of knowledge. Just before being released a few days before, each fish had been anesthetized and equipped with a transmitter the size of a cigarette filter, with a trailing eight-inch antenna. The transmitter is inserted into the fish's gullet using a ballpoint pen casing, and the antenna hangs out one side of the fish's mouth and trails behind. It looks very uncomfortable, but after a while the fish seem to get over it and resume their normal activity, although their longer-term survival is doubtful.

We were going to use a receiving antenna to locate our smolt. The transmitters were sending out a signature *click* every six seconds or so. Each transmitter's *click* had been previously logged into the receiver's database and assigned an identification number. The fish could then be individually tracked until the batteries wore out after about twenty days. The transmissions get considerably weaker if the fish descends to any great depths, but smolt don't tend to do that. They do, however, frequently get eaten by bigger fish, along with the $208 transmitter, but the biologists can almost always tell when that has happened, because the transmitter's movement suddenly changes. It goes deeper, sulks under a log, or scoots back into a weed bed.

We trailered a Boston Whaler out to the public boat launch above the dam and put in. Even though it was early in the season, the recreationists were already there. One of them must have just gotten a new toy, a big, snarling boat, and he was by himself near shore doing the aquatic equivalent of doughnuts, the boat rearing up and throwing a chaotic wake smashing against the shore. It was more than annoying; it made it harder to get our boat in. But for many, this is was what Fifteen Mile Falls had recently become. On summer weekends especially, the air would hang thick with exhaust fumes, and there would be a constant din of Jet Skis, water-skiers, and powerboats here. For the power crowd, this is what a reservoir is: the perfect recreational surface, whether here or at Lake Powell, serene and inviting as a golf course. Like a lawn in both appearance and sterility, it conveys a sense of security, of nature under control, of chaos kept at bay.

Fortunately Moore is also a big reservoir, and the people who increasingly come up from the urban areas downstream seem uneasy without each other's company. They seldom wander far from the launch, are discomforted by the looming hills, the vastness of it all. Tim sat in the bow wearing a headset and sweeping back and forth with the antenna while Brian steered us away from the boat launch and out over the sunken towns of Pattenville and Waterford. Whatever pain the flooding of those towns had caused, whatever tragedy lay below us in the silt-covered stone walls and foundations, and no matter how dead, cold, and oxygen deprived those dark waters may be, the reflection of sky made everything seem okay. You could feel the tension easing away as we put the noise behind us, and the broad blue waters and surrounding hills began to work their magic. Our helmsman began to munch fresh green asparagus from his garden while he steered; it was a communion of sorts with the springtime that surrounded us, although we exchanged worries that this spring was so dry, no rain in weeks now, rivers dropping fast.

We had only gone a few miles from the dam when we got our first hit. We slowed the boat and moved closer. It was number 94, on a lonely journey six miles from the headwaters where it had been put in. There was something magical about this for me, a fisherman who had spent many days on this body of water blindly trying to figure out what the fish were doing. This one was cruising southward a hundred feet or so beyond the bouldered shore, on a steady course. Did it know what it was doing, heading unerringly toward the sea, or was it more like Brownian motion as it experienced life outside a tank for the first time? There was no way of telling until we found the rest of the fish.

We chatted as we moved up the reservoir, circling into coves and out around headlands, the valley slowly narrowing. It was midmorning now, and the water had become almost like glass, reflecting steep hillsides that comprised unbroken forest except for the power line coming down from Hydro-Quebec. This power line is popular with the local marijuana growers, who live in the hills of adjacent Concord, Vermont, and seldom get caught. There are people living in cabins up in there who never pay a property tax at all because the town can't find them. There used to be people illegally camped along the shore here, too, just like Vietcong, and during our reconnaissance the summer before, we had come across the abandoned camps: a few tattered folding lounge chairs, some torn plastic tarps, a few soggy sleeping bags, and a lot of cans and bottles.

Tough country, and more foreboding as the channel necked down, with the hills on each side getting closer, darker. "I can hear the banjos playing," Cleve had said on our earlier excursions up there. Tim and Brian knew Warden Saunders, the man Drega had wounded. He used to work with them, but then decided to go into enforcement. They preferred this work, although here, too, there was always the chance encounter with the more militant members of the property rights movement. There aren't a lot of choices for young biologists just out of graduate school; you can work for the government or you can work for a consulting firm. They agreed that the private sector offered more freedom and opportunity for them to be objective, which surprised me. It was my first inkling that all was not as it was supposed to be. I would have guessed things to be the other way around, but anyway what mattered to Brian and Tim was the quality of the data, not how it might be interpreted by the men in suits later. Then we found the rest of the fish, still within a few hundred feet of where they had been put in, still waiting for the four o'clock feeding of Purina fish chow, so we went home.

8

It's only a matter of time, Indian, you can't sleep with the river forever.

— Leslie Marmon Silko

There are times on the river when the voices of the past can be heard along with the murmur of the current, but you have to listen carefully. Sometimes you can see traces, too; the plows turn up more every year as they comb through the fertile floodplain soil, and a friend found a circle of stone weights where a throwing net had been misplaced long ago. Bits of pottery and flints constantly fall from eroding banks, and an eerie figure carved in rock keeps watch over the river at Bellows Falls.

One of the places studied most intently during our relicensing process was Nine Islands, where the Passumpsic enters the Connecticut, just below Comerford Dam, just above the still waters of McIndoe. Even though the river rises and falls to a mechanical beat, even though the interstate highway is less than a mile away, and a railroad runs alongside, and power lines vault overhead, it is also one of the last relatively unspoiled remnants of what all of the river once was like — an island sanctuary, cut off by the vagaries of modern development. Here, there are riverside pines well over a hundred feet tall, and cathedral groves of silver maple, and here the hobbled waters still speak as they feel their way around the islands and through the boulder fields.

The largest of the islands, which the locals call Indian Island, stands like a fortress above the confluence. It is a high flat remnant of the postglacial peneplain, unlike the other, low floodplain islands. Shrouded in dark pine and hemlock, it is also a natural place to camp and watch for enemies coming down from the north or up from the south, and people have been doing so for at least ten thousand years, wearing footpaths deep into the clay. Only at night, after the south wind has died down, does the banshee wail of the interstate resound through the deep rift of the river to remind the dreamer. Otherwise it is easy to imagine a time when the water belonged to everyone, and you could drink from it no matter where you were.

This is a place to which I have come countless times, my favorite place on the river. Most of the times I have come here alone, in good times and bad, but I have also come with my family, with fishermen and photographers, with scientists and lovers and adventurers and government officials, and all have come back somehow improved by the experience. It is not just the message of the past here that the river conveys, but also the fragility of the present. There is a message, too, in the power lines that droop overhead, for they connect with a place not too far away where the rivers still run free, and Indians make their camps beside them.

In Canada it simply never was national policy to use the army or vigilantes to exterminate those who had what the whites wanted. There were no massacres, no so-called Indian Wars. There, the Native people were driven back in more subtle but still effective ways. Remnants remained, and remain today in places that whites don't want or have any use for. Much of the Canadian subarctic is such a place, where the boreal forest gives way to the taiga of dwarfed and relatively useless trees and where there is water, so much water running in all directions that from the air it looks like the glacier just melted yesterday and, relatively speaking, it did.

In 1991 I was given a magazine assignment to investigate the claims of those Northern Cree who had recently come down through Vermont much as their ancestors had. They said that the power line that had almost extinguished me and my boys on that sunny day at Comerford Reservoir was slowly extinguishing them, too. They came to public meetings in church basements and town halls all across Vermont telling us that the state should not buy power from Quebec. Meanwhile Hydro-Quebec, the provincially owned utility giant, was countering those claims by flying entire classes of Vermont schoolkids up to the Quebec frontier for the day, just so they could see for themselves what a wonderful thing Hydro-Quebec was doing for all of humankind including the Cree. There was a lot at stake: hundreds of millions in pending power contracts and, in the longer term, the energy future of both Quebec and New England.

For thousands of years the Northern Cree had lived pretty much the same way, just south of the Inuit who lived by the ice and north of the tribes of the deep woodlands. All through the times that we call "modern," through our great wars and the countless inventions with which we mark progress, the Northern Cree trapped fur. They would set out in small family groups in autumn, using the myriad waterways just as their ancestors on the Connecticut did, often traveling as much as two hundred miles to their hunting grounds. There, they would spend the incredibly long winter in a shelter. Once this was built of logs and hide, but over the past few hundred years or so they had adopted a square canvas tent from the Hudson's Bay Company topping a shoulder-high frame of logs chinked with moss, just as they have adopted the rifle, the steel trap, the teapot, and the iron stove.

Little else changed. In spring the family groups would wend their ways back down the waterways to the mouths of those great north-flowing rivers where "The Company" had its trading posts. They would stay there, celebrating sunlight and reunion through the short summer, while the furs began the journey south to our land, where they would adorn the heads and shoulders of white people. The village of Whapmagoostui, my ultimate destination, was just a small settlement of shacks at the mouth of the Great Whale River, and the trading post, and an Anglican church that was un-staffed through the winter. Then, in the early 1950s, the slumber was broken, first with the roar of bulldozers and then the scream of jet aircraft turbines. Almost overnight an airbase sprang up in the barren land next door to the village, part of the Distant Early Warning Line of the Cold War era.

The Cree moved closer, and many stopped trapping in winter as their prospects of freezing or starving to death were diminished by handouts. The Inuit moved south to cluster nearby, too. The government began to provide cheap housing and some food. For the first time, it was possible to watch television and feel stupid and deprived. Alcohol was more readily available. It was also possible to be in Montreal or Ottawa in a few hours if a medical emergency occurred, and it was even possible for a few to go away to college and learn things like law. Yet still, beside them as always was the Great Whale River, and still, in winter, most Cree families went up the narrowing tributaries to trap.

In the end it was the water itself that the white people came for. It was a political move as much as it was an economic one, for Quebec was being torn apart by the resurgent nationalism of the French, and Premier Robert Bourassa saw the development of the northern frontier as both a distraction and a promise of economic independence. Bulldozers began the long march northward through land that until then had been considered useless. In the 1980s they reached the La Grande River on James Bay, where the largest of many dams began producing fifteen times the output of Fifteen Mile Falls. They were in the process of rearranging the whole northern watershed of Canada's largest province. There were already rivers that once flowed east and now flowed west — to the turbines of Hydro-Quebec instead of the wilds of Labrador. There were immediate plans to flood an area the size of all New England, and long-term plans to export the water itself as far south as Chicago and the Mississippi.

Not only was Hydro-Quebec going to the public relations extreme of flying classes of schoolchildren up from Vermont to visit the La Grande complex for the day, but it was also offering free fishing trips to Vermont utility executives, legislators, and lawyers as it courted the lucrative contract. Several acquaintances of mine had returned from these treks with wide-eyed admiration for the pristine lakes in which trophy trout could be caught with little more than a shiny hook. This was not only one more affront to business ethics, but also yet one more affront to both the Cree and the fish. These sportsmen were not told that those lakes can only produce a pound of fish per acre a year, as compared to twenty pounds per acre in southern Quebec and fifty pounds in the States. The fish were indeed very big, very old, very naive about fishermen, and quickly gone.

......

Flying northward, it was possible to follow the strip of power lines and the access roads below almost all the way from Montreal, through the vast clear-cut and past open-pit mines, over hundreds of lakes and rivers, to La Grande, where we made a stop and went through a sort of security check. The airstrip there had the common military frontier feel, with lots of steel and plywood buildings and helicopters constantly coming and going. The Cree and Inuit among us were subjected to a rigorous customs inspection that smacked of racism as the agents turned their magnetometers on high and did strip searches for candy wrappers. The Indians in turn got even in their own little way by defacing the Hydro-Quebec posters on the plywood walls with their pens and fingernails. It was a cruel and raw place.

On the final leg of my journey the Inuit suddenly became excited and began to crowd the windows, because they could finally see great floes of ice on the bay below us. That was pretty much the last fun thing that happened for the next few days. The next airport was hardly even that — just a Quonset hut, and nobody was there to meet me, as had been promised. The people who were there, filled with the excitement of arrival or departure, paid no attention to me and would speak only Cree or Inuit. It was with great difficulty that I finally reached somebody in the village by phone, who begrudgingly agreed to find some sort of accommodations for me. I walked more than a mile across a barren, wind-blown landscape, the ice-choked bay to my right, sand, drab cubes of Inuit housing, and then more sand to my left. Although it was early June, a fine steady snow was blowing in off the bay.

In retrospect it should not have surprised me that these people don't generally welcome white strangers into their midst. But in a relationship that was always adversarial, the

Cree of Whapmagoostui had managed to parlay their claims into a village of modern suburban-style houses out on that otherwise vacant coastal plain. Even though many of the houses still had tepees pitched out front, where many Cree preferred to live in summer, each family also had a fine three-bedroom home, with a finished basement, wall-to-wall carpeting, a modern kitchen, and two baths. They had some of the first cell phones and satellite TVs in Canada. I was less prepared for that than I was for the cool reception.

I was incarcerated in the basement guest room of my host family. The host himself began demanding money whenever his wife was out of earshot. Otherwise he lay on the living room sofa in his bikini underwear all day watching professional wrestling on television, waiting for the ongoing tribal party to resume. What a party it was! The whole tribe had just returned from "goose camp," which was but one of the many social events that filled their summer. The best hunters among them had intercepted upward of a hundred geese each for the village larder as the birds came in for a landing after their long northward migration. Generally the partying started at about four or five in the afternoon with a lot of excited preliminary conversations on the cell phones, and lasted all the way through the short night, punctuated by yelling and occasional shotgun blasts. Things didn't begin to simmer down until well after sunrise the next day, which was at two A.M. I was never invited.

At first, I was so miserable that I explored the possibility of chartering a plane to come and get me before the next scheduled flight out. I went for long walks, and bought cans of horrible food at the company store. It was worse than dog food — just fat and fillers and food dye, but with deceptive labels like DINTY MOORE. Then slowly, starting with the children, I began to make friends. My hostess, a very kind and gentle woman, took pity on me and served me the traditional goose roasted on an open fire. Some of the old trappers agreed to meet with me, and a young woman went along as my translator. Gradually the village began to open like an Arctic flower, shy and delicate in a harsh land.

Back and forth I went, crossing the sandy plain between houses, while everyone in the village kept track of me by cell phone. I began to realize that this was more a tightly knit family than what we would think of as a village, and underlying the traditional celebration and reunion that summer brought there was also a deep anxiety about their traditional way of life. Perhaps it was true that "their way of life is finished anyway," as the officials of Hydro-Quebec liked to say, but this is always the excuse worldwide, making extermination somehow seem more acceptable as a sort of cultural euthanasia.

We would start each interview with some tea, which was always on the stove in every home. There were also always several generations present, gathering shyly to listen, youngest closest to us. Joseph Petagumskum and his sons had shot eighty-six geese the week before, but he was worried that there were not as many this year, and that the helicopters were keeping them away. He showed me a photograph taken in 1936, when he was just two, of his father as a young, strong, and happy man kneeling beside a freshwater seal he had just shot while guiding white people. Joseph was worried that the few freshwater seals now remaining would die because of the flooding and mercury poisoning. Mercury had just been found in the flooded waters, making the fish unsafe to eat and causing early symptoms of poisoning among some Cree people.

Weemish Mamianskum said that the seals could crawl up to half a mile overland and hoped some would relocate, but he was not willing to relocate himself. He had been born in the bush and trapped along the same low-lying waterways as his father had. He had been on the public relations tour through Vermont, and while it was interesting he missed his home and the store food always left him feeling hungry. Nothing was as nourishing as wild food — it was a spiritual fulfilment and connection, too — and the mercury was a very bad sign. This sentiment was echoed by Andrew Natachequan. Andrew made the traditional snowshoes, and he had them hanging above him as he spoke. They were almost round, and as finely woven as Belgian lace. He said he would still keep trapping, even though he was sixty-six and nearly all of his territory was going to be flooded. Like many of the older Cree, he thought that the mercury came from the flooded graves of his ancestors, and added that this had all been foretold to him by a seer many decades ago.

William Kawapit also agreed that the mercury was a spiritual thing. Then he got out his topographic map and moved his tan, leathery hand across it with a caressing motion, a gliding movement as though his hand were a canoe. His hand paused at each place where an ancestor had died and been buried in the bush, then moved on to show me the good fishing places, the places where the geese landed to feed, the portages to the next lake, and the next and the next. Of course he didn't need the map to find his own way; a duplicate copy existed in his head.

I was invited to visit the school and talk to some of the children. Like the houses, the school was modern and well equipped, and I was immediately welcomed as a real live show-and-tell. As impressed as I had been by the depth of the elders, I was simply delighted by the innate curiosity of the children. Their curriculum was finally back in their own hands, after generations of sanctimonious condescension from Ottawa, and it was leaning heavily into science, environmentalism, and cultural awareness. This was more than a spark of hope. It was a potential bonfire.

Finally, after a week, the young male leaders acknowledged my existence and spoke to me. They were the ones who had gone away to school, organized the publicity tours, and instigated legal actions. They were aware of the movement toward utility deregulation in the States, and what it could mean, long before we were. They were the warriors. Dave Masty, the band's director of operations, said it best. "The Cree are a peaceful nation," he told me as we sat in a circle at the kitchen table. "We never had to fight for our territory. We are also a Christian people, and we believe in living in harmony with nature and people. But also, 60 percent of our people are under thirty, more educated, better informed about the treatment of Native people in the past, more proud of our culture, more militant, more outraged." They were not holding out for another settlement. They just wanted the flooding to stop.

In the long pink evenings, while the Cree partied, I would walk up to the highlands east of the village. Here was our earth, so raw and vast. There was the pack ice out there, a glowing white streak by the gray stones of the Manitounuk Islands, and the broad outwash plain below. There were young people dashing back and forth on their ATVs, long black hair trailing back in the wind, in the throes of courtship and adventure. Here and there a plume of smoke curled upward from an outlying camp, with its floor of sweet-scented spruce bows, and tea on the stove.

There were more trees as the land began to rise toward me, though mostly just shoulder high, following the defiles between rough shoulders of lichen-encrusted rock; spruce, balsam, and the larch with its bright green needles just beginning to emerge. To the south lay the river, enormous, half a mile wide, roiling with snowmelt, steep banks of sand on both sides, popular with beluga whales — but I was finding it hard to love it myself, and was ready to return to my place near the Connecticut. This was such a vast and harsh land, theirs to love, not mine, and they were doing a better job of it than we were.

They still had the two most precious things life offers anywhere: a deep connection to the mystery of life itself, and a deep connection to each other. And these two things are precisely what our "modern" American culture is destroying. If the Cree could keep the alcohol under control, which is a constant painful struggle, they would succeed where we are failing. Technology is a good thing. Knowledge is even better. Wisdom is best of all, but it can't exist when the spiritual and personal connections are lost, and we drift like dust in the wind of advertisers, politicians, and religious zealots.

The worldwide destruction of traditional cultures is just as much of an uncontrolled experiment as global warming is, with equally dire consequences in the longer term, but long terms are irrelevant in a world of immediate gratification. In the rush toward "globalization," which is in fact exactly the opposite, few things seem to attract both politicians and investment bankers better than big dam building, whether in Quebec or Brazil or Egypt or China, and Hydro-Quebec was counting on both utility deregulation and the peak summertime demand of air-conditioning in the northeastern United States for its future profits. It was our air-conditioning — which makes global warming not only tolerable but also marketable, the narcotic of air-conditioning that seductively puts the environment into an even more deeply adversarial role — that was flooding the land of the Cree. And it was clear to the Cree that the weather was changing. The permafrost was melting. The lichens that the reindeer ate were being replaced by grasses and sedge. While I was walking the headlands a few days before I left, the temperature soared thirty degrees and I was caught in a tremendous thunderstorm.

I finally got invited to a party. The night before I was flying out there was going to be a celebration of a successful "cleanup week" of picking up the dregs of winter. I was looking forward to it. But then a young Inuit in the neighboring village of Kuujjuarapik committed suicide, and both villages went into mourning. One supposes it was alcohol again, for this is the great scourge, worse than smallpox, and one that similarly found the people genetically unprepared. As I got ready to leave, I remembered a Cree word that I had overheard and asked Linda, my interpreter, about it: *wachiya*. She said it was the Cree word for "hello" and also "good-bye." But Maggie, my hostess, said she didn't think there really was a Cree word for "good-bye."

In the article that resulted from my trip I concluded that not only was the proposed power contract bad business, but it might also be dishonest business. It was a conclusion the magazine deemed unprintable, but it has largely been accepted in the decade that has elapsed since then, obligated to the infamous contract. The Cree of Whapmagoostui have managed to keep the dam builders at bay, but as Merrill Lynch continued to solicit bids for the generating facilities of New England Power through 1997 and '98, the dam workers at Fifteen Mile Falls overheard a lot of French being spoken by dark-suited visitors. It seemed like a perfect deal for Hydro-Quebec, for they already had an entryway into our market through that big fat DC line. But when the bids were finally opened, the winner was Pacific Gas and Electric, another behemoth and the legendary sparring partner of both David Brower and Erin Brockovich.

9

Freedom of the press is guaranteed only to those who own one.

— A. J. Liebling

The best way to see how a river defines a landscape is by air, not canoe. Flying above the Great Whale, or the Mekong, or the Connecticut, or any of the rivers that lace our continent from New York to Los Angeles, one can see how our civilizations have followed their path. One can see their crenellated beginnings in the shadows of mountainsides, and their slow, lethargic end in the fractal curlicues of estuaries. Our highways, our railways, and our towns nestle beside them. Our farms are defined by them. They carry us, along with water and soil.

Earthbound and in the canoe again, one can still see how a river unifies, giving focus to a watershed. It provides a commonality of habitat and topography, and orientation for both the landscape and the traveler. A river has a song of its own, which can be heard on both shores equally. And yet a river can also divide, serving as a barrier to communication or as a line of defense or demarcation. In these two abilities, to either unify or divide, it might be said that politicians can resemble rivers, and rivers politicians as they negotiate their way toward the sea, finding compromise and common ground between obstinate hills. All too often, though, and especially in a society that has lost its spiritual and social connections, it is the politics of greed and self-aggrandizement that prevails, and the result simply resembles a swamp.

Never was this more clear than after the relicensing settlement for Fifteen Mile Falls had been hammered out. Like all settlements it was a compromise between interested parties, and between two states as well, for the Upper Connecticut also serves as the boundary between New Hampshire and Vermont, two staunchly New England states that share both common traits and certain differences. Some of these differences date back to before the American Revolution, and a time when ownership of the land was disputed between New Hampshire and New York. Vermont opportunistically came in to fill the breach, but the squabble really began between two continents long ago, when what is now Africa crashed into North America, then drifted apart again, leaving a rift of jolted stone that the river now runs through.

Most of our negotiations for a new hydroelectric operating license took place in New Hampshire, at what had once been a hilltop estate called The Rocks. The regional planning agency and several other public groups had set up offices there when the former owners donated their extensive holdings, and it was a comfortable and attractive setting for our long and often hotly contested sessions. The rocks for which the estate had been named were extraordinary. Great fields of granite boulders had been transformed into four-foot-wide stone walls, and many of the turn-of-the-twentieth-century buildings had walls made of stones the size of grand pianos. New Hampshire is, after all, the Granite State, largely under-

lain by the obdurate mineral that resisted the scour of the glaciers relatively well, with the White Mountains particularly
standing out on the horizon as an example.

This geology limited the possibilities for agriculture. What
soil there was between the stones tended to be sandy and
acidic, better suited to growing timber, while the steep hills
and plunging streams made excellent mill sites. Manufacturing and the timber industry became the dominant
economies, and these businesses do not welcome government
planning or regulation. The environment, while welcome
enough, is mainly a resource to be developed. This is readily
apparent as one drives the river valley, crossing back and forth
between states. There is little regulation of roadside advertising in New Hampshire, and zoning is nearly absent in the
New Hampshire towns of the Upper Valley, being perceived as
one of the most egregious examples of the loss of property
rights. While Vermont villages remain relatively compact and
neat, those on the New Hampshire side of the river have often
lost their center, with businesses and residences meandering
across abandoned farms and woodlots. Trailer parks and
shopping centers are welcomed, and often locate in the floodplains at the river's edge, attracting displaced Vermonters.

Vermont, on the other hand, is largely underlain by softer
and sweeter derivatives of limestone. There are still hills, to
be sure, but of the more gentle and rounded type, while the
soils are loamy and fertile. It was the perfect place for the
patchwork of small farms that soon came to characterize this
state where the cows outnumbered people by a long shot, and
if you expand the census to all livestock, people are still outnumbered today. But when the small farm began to decline in
the 1920s and 1930s, it became increasingly clear that
Vermont was in trouble. The state began to develop a tourism
industry and, in 1946, started publishing *Vermont Life*, the

first state tourism magazine in the nation. It portrayed a romantic place with white clapboard villages and rolling farmscapes, where friendly people in checkered shirts made maple syrup, cheese, and crafts. It attracted people like me, flatlanders who grew up in the rootless suburbs and were not tied to a cow's tail. We had the professional and economic advantage of being able to choose where we wanted to live, and we chose Vermont, asserting ourselves into the community. Before long, the state began to hold itself to the image it had created, imposing ever more stringent environmental and development controls. We liked it, with many taking government jobs, while local resentment often simmered unnoticed.

In the parking lot of The Rocks, the license plates proclaiming GREEN MOUNTAIN STATE so far outnumbered New Hampshire's LIVE FREE OR DIE that to many it seemed the greens had taken over and were driving the process, even though New Hampshire owned most of the river, with the boundary being at the high-water mark on the Vermont side. Our governor played an active role, his awareness heightened by our canoe trips, although much of the time his role was more to keep the greens reined in a bit. We got the governor of New Hampshire in a canoe a few times, too. As both a Democrat and a woman, Governor Jean Shaheen was never popular in the northern part of the state, and the fact that she was actually seen on the river in the same canoe as the governor of Vermont was perceived by many as treasonous. While the federal operating license for the dams on the river was being negotiated, and for quite a while afterward, the press remained ominously silent. But it was only a matter of days after the public formal signing and photo opportunity with both governors that the politicians of New Hampshire struck back, publicly denouncing the agreement, and canoes as well, in a number of prominent editorials.

The timing was carefully calculated, for — geology aside — New Hampshire politics are also fired to a white heat by the state's habit of holding an early presidential primary. The early primary turns even the small-town cranks into king-makers, or breakers. They can bring strong men to tears and leave weak ones standing. It is a contact sport in which no holds are barred, and it goes into overtime in the north. So with an eye toward potential real estate development, as well as potential votes, several New Hampshire legislators and soon-to-be candidates exploded with feigned rage, crying out to the public that they were being robbed, that taxpayers were footing the bill to create a park for canoeing environ-mentalists, and that motorboats and snowmobiles would be banned from the river and surrounding lands.

Call it "politics by arson," a common enough tactic: Light the fire and then claim to be the only one who can put it out. The "facts" in the editorials were largely the fabrication of a corpulent pin-striped attorney from nearby Littleton, New Hampshire, with political ambitions. He went on for nearly five thousand words, rambling in and out of coherency. It ran most prominently in a newspaper published in neighboring St. Johnsbury, Vermont, the same paper that had given Carl Drega a degree of approval earlier. Editors found it suffi-ciently newsworthy to run it on the front page for two con-secutive days. Shortly thereafter, the lawyer from Littleton announced his legislative candidacy, and that November he was elected, of course. Meanwhile the St. Johnsbury newspa-per continued to pay almost no attention at all to the steady intimidation of local towns by the lawyers of Pacific Gas and Electric as they negotiated their property assessments down-ward still farther in the name of free-market economy, play-ing one town against the other and insisting on secrecy.

Disheartening as these riverbank shenanigans were, however, the ones on the banks of the Potomac were worse. There, it was President Clinton, a Democrat who had made promises to the environmental movement, versus a Republican Congress that had made promises to the property rights movement. No significant legislation was able to breach this deadlock, so Clinton strategists focused instead on his Council on Environmental Quality. As a presidential council this body's role was purely advisory. Members had no legislative powers, but they could be useful in what really was more of a marketing strategy, using existing laws and a lot of spin to create at least the illusion of activism.

The American Heritage Rivers initiative was announced by Clinton in his 1997 State of the Union address. Ten rivers would be selected as Heritage Rivers, and each would receive special assistance from an interagency task force to promote and improve the environmental, economic, historic, and cultural aspect of the river and its river-based communities. Such improvement of a watershed is a good thing, but this was based on favoritism from the start. The promise of pork met a predictable response: Environmental groups began to stumble over each other in the rush to get their local river nominated, and the property rights activists screamed that this was another attempted land grab, circumventing Congress and the laws of the nation to put more restrictions on loggers and farmers.

Byzantium herself could not have seen anything more convoluted than the path of this bit of nonlegislation through Congress and court. But while in Washington this was but one of many bits of chum for the feeding frenzy of lawyers, for us on the Connecticut it was simply a pain in the ass. Forced to choose between being one of "us" and one of "them," our river advisory commission reluctantly chose "us" — of course, for it is also an unwritten law that the whiff of pork, no matter how distant, is always worth a closer look. Meanwhile the field of choices nationally was narrowing. It was decided that any river that ran through the district of a congressman who opposed the initiative would be automatically disqualified. That limited the choices among western rivers in particular. But what about a really big and important river like the Mississippi? Just because of some staunchly opposed representatives, do you let the whole thing go, Mark Twain and all? No, you make more exceptions. Parts of really big rivers can qualify, just not the parts that go through those unrelenting districts.

And so it went, for another year. The nomination document for the Connecticut itself was heavy as a doorstop, the product of endless meetings and compromises among groups with some very basic underlying differences. There was something repulsive about it from the start, this organizing of a beauty contest, a publicity stunt that had nothing to do with science, or economics, or the needs of both rivers and societies themselves. Yet some of us (not me) had to pretend that this was something wonderful and magnificent, a real breakthrough that could lead to a lot of other nonlegislative environmental initiatives. Others (me) simply suffered in silence while the hucksters took over. When the envelopes were finally opened late in the summer of 1998 the winner was the Connecticut, along with thirteen others, because the field had been widened again and the rules changed to accommodate all the really good districts. Exuberant press releases fluttered through the mails.

Another publicity effort was launched to nominate the Connecticut River as one of America's Most Endangered Rivers. Applications were solicited by the American Rivers advocacy group, and activists downstream responded, angry that the river was now largely controlled by an even more remote owner that was manipulating the flows for its own profit while exporting the energy generated and strangling the tax base of riverside towns. There were also some efforts in downstream towns where dams were located to actually buy the hydroelectric facilities from Pacific Gas and Electric, claiming that the river was part of the "commons" and invoking the ancient and besieged concept of "public trust." None of these efforts got far, however. There was little support in the legislatures and none locally where the relicensing settlement had just been signed, where "public trust" was trusted even less than government, and where hope remained that things would get better under the new license terms.

Meanwhile, editorials and letters to the editor crashed back and forth like mortar rounds, mostly coming from the right against what was, in their minds by now, the Great Canoe Conspiracy. Evidence of the conspiracy had begun to emerge during our canoe trips with Vermont's governor, evidence that was not hard to gather given that the press was often invited, but which became more damning when the "traitorous" governor of New Hampshire joined us for a mile or two. Further proof came when our commission reflected the concerns of local residents and cautioned against the environmental impacts of a new motorized boating access proposed in a conservation area. That was enough for some New Hampshire lawmakers to grumble about disbanding their side of the commission entirely. Now anybody with a canoe was suspect.

I had to go canoeing just to get away from it all.

It was turning out to be another very dry year. After the driest May on record, the streams had reached their midsummer low levels. In mid-June the bass season opened and I went canoeing on the blue waters of Comerford Reservior with my middle son, who was visiting for a week. As always, it was exquisitely beautiful; the broad glittering lake leading the eye to the distant horizon, the hills fading from green to gray, the sweet-scented forest slipping by on the near shore, people looking at us suspiciously on the far shore.

This was a pilgrimage for us — familiar waters where my children had learned to swim and fish and canoe. It was a time for the two of us to share in near silence; we always tried to come on weekdays when there are fewer powerboats and we had the water nearly to ourselves. We had assumed that this time, because of the growing drought, the water would be low, exposing the sandbars and beaches that made fishing from shore more fun. We had spent many days on that sand, watching the colors of the hills across the lake change as the sun went down.

But this time the water was unusually high. It was so high, in fact, that it was up in the vegetation along the banks. Clumps of vegetation were sloughing off the banks and falling into the reservoir. The water along the edges was murky with wave-washed sediment. There were clumps of vegetation floating offshore. There were even trees sliding into the reservoir. Predictably, the fishing was terrible. But sometimes the fishing is good below the dam, and anyway we were curious about what was going on. We landed and walked down a long path beside the dizzying concrete wall and buttresses.

The water behind the dam was so high that there were pressure leaks springing out all over the dam's face. A pretty good flow of water was coursing down over the rocks of what was once Mulliken's Pitch just from the leaks, but otherwise the tailrace pool was still. The dam was still holding its water back, seemingly about to burst from the strain. The rocks in the riverbed were dry, the river itself watered only by the leaks. Many hours had passed with no water coming forth, and many more hours were to come. I was very familiar with the dam's operating regime, and this was something I had never seen before.

Then it came to me. They were playing the spot market for electricity. In the newly deregulated energy market, utilities were now bidding for power purchased at a price that could change every five minutes, just like the traditional commodities brokers on the Chicago Mercantile Exchange. The dam owners were waiting for the price to get even higher, during this hot and unusually dry year, waiting for all the air conditioners in Springfield and Holyoke to come on. Only then, when the price had reached ten or even twenty times the usual rate, would the golden gallons be allowed to pour forth. A year later Cleve told me that on one of those afternoons during that time of heat and drought, the company made as much money in six hours as it had during the rest of the entire year.

Two more years would elapse between the time that the terms of the new license were agreed upon and the time that the new license was issued. Meanwhile the company was free to experiment with flows, testing the waters (so to speak) in the brave new world of energy speculation. This was a new game, one all of us were just learning, with a few big winners and lots of losers. Enron was playing it, too. It could hold back water, or hold back the electricity itself, as it would soon be doing in California, blaming the environmentalists and government regulation all the time. In the end Pacific Gas and Electric would be one of the biggest losers of all. Besides the public and the environment, that is, and through it all the press just kept fulminating about liberals and canoes.

10

> *People of the same trade seldom meet together, even for merriment and diversion, but the conversation ends in a conspiracy against the public, or in some contrivance to raise prices.*
>
> — Adam Smith

While exquisitely beautiful, there is also something deceptive about the way our planet looks from space. Of that great blueness, of that wealth of water that so distinguishes our planet from all others we know of, only a very little bit is the pure fresh water of our lakes and rivers. More than 97 percent is the saline solution of our oceans. Of that which is left, most by far is frozen in ice caps and glaciers. There is just one teaspoon of liquid fresh water on the surface of our planet for every thirteen gallons elsewhere, and it is by no means evenly distributed. About forty-four inches of fresh solar-distilled water falls upon New England every year, but the average for the United States is less than thirteen inches, and many places receive far less than that.

Welcome to Las Vegas. In a nation that was founded by real estate developers and religious fanatics, this is surely the promised land. Water has made the desert bloom, water and air-conditioning, here and elsewhere across the Southwest,

where golf courses have become one of water's largest consumers. Municipal Water District Commissions and Water
Authorities often wield more power than elected officials. In
cites such as Las Vegas, Reno, Carson City, Albuquerque,
Denver, Houston, Salt Lake City, and Flagstaff, real estate
development is outpacing the development of new water supplies. Bitter fights among the water interests of agriculture,
real estate, and environmental causes are escalating. The
Colorado River is so hammered by impoundments and withdrawals that at times during the year it fails to reach the sea.
Lake Mead, which lies above the ancient canyons like a giant
dead blue lizard, is at its lowest level in thirty years. In other
parts of the world, things are considerably worse.

It is no wonder, then, that some have called water "the oil
of the twenty-first century," and are making water the next
big target for deregulation and privatization worldwide.
Multinationals such as RWE Thames and Vivendi are already
aggressively buying up water rights in the United States.
Those rights are traded and speculated on just like any other
commodity, but the market is held captive. This is an irre-
sistible opportunity for profit, and of course Hydro-Quebec
saw this coming years ago, too, with its plan for a canal to
the Midwest. Those of us in the water-rich Northeast, however, have remained blissfully unaware of water's growing
scarcity except during far more isolated episodes of drought.
The Connecticut still reaches the sea.

There is more to a river's flow than simply whether it does
or doesn't, however. Just as in other complex systems such as
rain forests or coral reefs, a grand and interconnected variety
of organisms have evolved with the rivers themselves, which
depend on the magnitude, frequency, duration, and timing of
a river's flows. This dependence and connectedness begins
below the river, in the saturated sediments colonized by

microorganisms — the shredders and decomposers — and ascends through the evolutionary ladder from algae and zooplankton to insects and their larvae, fish, amphibians, and the great umbrella of riverside trees.

Flows themselves depend on weather and the topography of the watershed. Steep upland streams with shallow soils tend to be "flashy," rising and falling fast within hours of a precipitation event, while the great lowland river responds more lethargically. In the most general terms, about half of the rain that falls becomes runoff and enters the surface waters — more when the ground is frozen or already saturated, less when it is dry and especially less when summer foliage quickly transpires moisture back into the air again. In New England 55 percent of an average river's flow occurs in springtime, 12 in summer, 14 in fall, and 10 percent in winter. These seasonal norms are of course full of spikes and troughs as dry high-pressure systems, coastal lows, and frontal systems parade overhead. The river reflects both the weather above it and the weather upstream, and the life within the river and along its shores responds in concert. What may seem to humankind to be chaotic extremes are but the river's great beating heart. Floods cleanse and nourish. Droughts purify with Spartan habitat, winnowing out intruders. Flow is what gives a river its voice, sometimes soft, sometimes deafening. Flow enriches the river's life.

It is in the river's edge environment, as it is in the edges of other systems, that the variety of life is both the richest and the most sensitive to disturbance. It is in the edge, where the waters rise and fall, that eggs are most likely incubated, that larvae emerge, that seeds sprout, each species having evolved in synchrony with the river's rise and fall. When that flow is manipulated — when the magnitude, frequency, duration, and timing of flows are changed by the many uses of humankind such as dams for power generation or recreation, or water withdrawals for industrial uses, irrigation, or snow-making — there are ripple effects throughout the ecosystem that are only now beginning to be understood. Aside from the well-known cleansing and renewal of extremely high flows, there are also ecosystem benefits from extremely low flows, such as the elimination of invasive species. But few species can thrive in a river that experiences both high flows and low flows several times a day.

Flow was also the subject of a report our organization commissioned called *Instream Flow Uses, Values and Policies in the Upper Connecticut River Watershed*. It was a thorough but general investigation of the subject, informative on the present regulatory environment and calling for coordination of efforts between the two states. Unfortunately, we inadvertently chose to present the report to the commissioners during the same meeting at which Cleve, our commissioner representing the power company, had chosen to present his new bosses. I think Cleve went first. I can't remember the names of the three higher executives he introduced; even the company itself was changing its own name periodically by then, like some backstreet bunko artist. At any rate, each of the company goons said a few words meant to be warm and reassuring, and then sat and resumed an expression of indifference.

The expressions on the goons' faces began to change, however, as the flow report was presented. While Cleve continued to smile and nod naively, the executives beside him turned pale, clenched their jaws, and began to squirm. It looked like they were about to jump up and leave the room before we mercifully took a break, and when they all came filing back in again, Cleve, too, was looking miserable, as though his three bosses had taken turns beating him up in the back alley. From then on, *flow* was not a word that could be uttered in

Cleve's presence without him launching into a long condemnation of the report and its implications.

Despite the name changes and disclaimers, this was still Pacific Gas and Electric; it has long been engaged in bitter battles out West over flow, and especially how flow affects the lives of salmon. Furthermore, its eastern entity on the Connecticut, whatever its name was at the time, had just been coerced by the U.S. Fish and Wildlife Service into putting radio transmitter tags on ten Atlantic salmon as they returned upstream that spring, and those fish were now headed toward the company dams, beeping like smart bombs along the way, because the terms of the utility's operating license required it to implement upstream fish passage as soon as a set number of salmon returned.

Among them was one known as number 42. She had made her way through the river's lower reaches, where the saline tongue of the sea reaches far inland, and ersatz castles sit upon the hills, and vast estates run their lawns down to the river's bank. She had passed the tank farms and shopping malls of Middletown and Hartford, and run the rapids of Enfield. The first real barrier she had encountered was the dam at Holyoke. There, a fish elevator has been installed by the owners. Fish seeking upstream passage are lured into a trap by an "attraction flow" of water, and then lifted up and over the dam. Along with giving the fish access upstream, it also gives fisheries biologists their first chance to assess the season's migration. On the sixth day of May, 1999, they trapped a salmon of striking size and beauty. She was carefully netted out and examined. She weighed nineteen pounds and was thirty-seven inches long. A scale was removed to determine her age. Then she was anesthetized, and a transmitter the size of a finger was surgically implanted in her abdomen courtesy of the U.S. Fish and Wildlife Service and PG&E.

She was assigned her number, allowed to recover, and replaced in the river.

Receiving antennas tracked her through the next fish ladders at Turners Falls, then Vernon, Vermont, where Jay, the state's biologist, picked up her signal by driving up and down the river holding a receiving antenna out the window of his truck. I had known Jay from years back, when I had done a piece on fish passage for ETV. What impressed me most back then was how much he really cared about his fish; he wasn't about to stress them by handling them too much just so that I could get a good shot. Each fish, shad in that case, was far more important to him than my show was, and in retrospect I have to admit he was right.

Jay followed number 42, and she followed her instincts, turning up into the West River just above Brattleboro, and then ascending to a pool below the Townshend flood control dam, where she loitered, resting for a while. On June 4 she entered a fish trap at the foot of the dam. She was netted, placed in an opaque "salmon bag," and driven by truck up around the high dam, much as it was proposed to do with salmon at the dams of Fifteen Mile Falls. Then, just upstream of the dam, she disappeared. Jay drove up and down the West River watershed for days, fretting that she may have been caught by a fisherman, who had then panicked, aware of the serious nature of his crime, and destroyed both the salmon and the transmitter. Perhaps the fish had been fatally injured during her capture and trip around the dam, or during the surgical implant. She could have perished on her own, as the water levels sank lower and lower in the increasingly severe drought. Already there were reports of die-offs, of fish going belly-up as what water there was left got too warm and too low in oxygen. In the past, fish with transmitters had been traced to landfills, the stomachs of bears, and the freezers of poachers, but this one seemed to have simply vanished without a trace, leaving a gaping void instead of a high point in Jay's career. In the past he would sometimes snorkel with his returning salmon just to know better what they knew, and this exceptionally large and genetically well-endowed specimen was the embodiment of a lifetime of work.

Such focus on a single species by a scientist is largely unfathomable to the public at large, to whom science itself is a bore if not downright suspicious. Science, too, suffers because of our present-day disconnect from the mysteries of life, the very mysteries scientists themselves love to solve. While Jay and others like him continue on their own personal quest, their work is too often twisted or misinterpreted. On the Connecticut, as elsewhere, both scientists and the public are often left out at the end of a whipsaw wielded by lawyers, politicians, and special interests. This, too, is part of our own painful evolution as a species. Progress is sure but unsteady.

On the Connecticut River many species besides the Atlantic salmon have become extirpated or are in danger of extinction, but they lack the public appeal. A shortnose sturgeon can't leap twelve feet into the air, and nobody is willing to spend thousands of dollars for the thrill of catching a dwarf wedge mussel. It took the Endangered Species Act of 1973, and the vision of our planet that led up to it, to improve the odds of those species in the appropriations game. The first big test of the act came in a contest with the federal government itself, where the Tennessee Valley

Authority was building a dam on the Little Tennessee River.

The Tellico Dam project was comparable to the hydroelectric projects on the Connecticut, with the notable exception that it was publicly, not privately, funded. Similar promises were made, assuring that the benefits of increased employment, electrical power, flood control, and recreational opportunities far outweighed the costs, including loss of habitat and property. With the Tellico project there was the additional business benefit of improved barge navigation, and construction began shortly after the funding was approved in 1966, much to the dismay of many environmentalists who disputed the cost–benefit analysis and saw the project as a boondoggle that would benefit only a few, at a large ecological cost.

When the three-inch-long snail darter made its international debut in the Little Tennessee, the language of the Endangered Species Act held up, and the project came to a halt. That the fine points of the law, and an otherwise undistinguished fish, had such economic power was to many a sore point that lingers to this day. To them this seemed like an instance of eco-extremism, and it set the stage for many battles to come, driving a wedge between science and business interests, dividing even the government itself, and adding still more fuel to the fiery rhetoric of politicians. Eventually snail darters were also discovered in nearby streams and the dam project resumed, but this discovery was more a matter of emerging science than compromise, and within a few more years the spotted owl would assume center stage as this fundamental battle continued.

Laws, like science, are constantly evolving, and both are equally deserving of respect. In Maine, where the natural returns of Atlantic salmon had been dramatically decreasing through the 1990s, there was increasing pressure to list the species as endangered. Timber companies and blueberry growers fought back, and for a while the effort stalled but eventually succeeded. On the Connecticut, where salmon had already disappeared and were now being restored, the language of the Endangered Species Act doesn't apply, but the 1965 Anadromous Fish Conservation Act does, and so does the Federal Power Act of 1986. As the renewal time for each federally licensed dam in the watershed grows closer, wildlife biologists within various state and federal agencies insist on language within the new license that would require fish passage, both upstream and down, either immediately or at a date to be determined.

Dam owners above Fifteen Mile Falls in particular were incensed. They knew that there were no anadromous fish above the falls, and saw the stocking of salmon fry and smolt upstream as a deliberate effort to force the issue, in defiance of both science and economics. Fisheries biologists, however, saw each new license as an opportunity that would not come up again for forty years, which is the usual license period. Even without the Endangered Species Act, the Atlantic salmon was being used as a weapon of confrontation as the environmental impact of dams became an increasing focus for activists. It was David Brower himself who first took on Pacific Gas and Electric for building dams in California, and the battle has broadened into the mainstream since. For better or worse, the salmon has joined the snail darter and the spotted owl in the pantheon of environmental law.

Hydrogenerating utilities like to point to the alternatives such as nuclear and coal-burning plants, which pollute the air and generate radioactive waste. They ask sarcastically which one environmentalists would prefer (while generally ignoring energy conservation), and the anti-dam lobby is often slapped with the stigma of elitism. At Fifteen Mile Falls and elsewhere, environmentalists are characterized as rich-kid kayakers and canoeists who want the river to themselves and couldn't care less about Joe Sixpack, who likes the reservoir for his powerboat and Jet Ski. As the rift deepens and becomes emotionally charged, dams become symbolic of a deeper social divide. What was once a recreational choice, whether to go canoeing or waterskiing, becomes a political choice as well.

Today the power crowd is clearly in control, to the point that the Equal Rights Amendment and the Americans with Disabilities Act are being used to demand access to wilderness areas by motorized recreation advocates and the industries they support. The American flag is with them wherever they go, pasted on windshields and helmets. What was once the symbol of intellectual freedom has become exactly the opposite. Scientists are left to fend for themselves or, worse, fend with each other, for in a complex watershed, as in any complex system, victory for one group of fisheries biologists might spell defeat for another. There is competition for habitat as well as for funding. Restoration of one species often comes at the expense of another. Some said a successful restoration of the striped bass was causing the salmon's decline. Others blamed the introduction of brown and rainbow trout.

Yet Atlantic salmon runs were dropping off dramatically all across their range, not just on the Connecticut. Runs in Maine, New Brunswick, and Northern Europe have been declining precipitously. Federally, emphasis finally began to shift toward protecting the existing wild stocks, while pressure mounted on the Connecticut program along with criticism. Budget requests were being pared back more and more. Federally subsidized vacancies at state hatcheries were going unfilled; technical improvements to hatcheries were being delayed.

Lacking an explanation for the worldwide decline, the short-term answer at the U.S. Fish and Wildlife's Connecticut River Atlantic salmon restoration headquarters seemed to be better public relations, which can be taken as a bad sign in itself. As with NASA's space shuttle program, there would be more projects with schoolchildren, more kits for teachers, more junkets with the press and legislators. Well intended as it all may have been, the restoration program seemed to be headed down the same well-trodden path of other bureaucracies, unable to retrench and impossible to stop.

Meanwhile, management of the Connecticut River's three animal species that really were endangered was proceeding quietly and largely successfully. The peregrine falcon was doing the best, and certainly was the easiest to market to the public. The banning of DDT, federal protection, and modest breeding programs had dozens of pairs nesting in the rock cliffs of the Connecticut's shores. The shortnose sturgeon is not nearly so photogenic, and spends most of its life out of sight in deep murky waters, much as it has for the last hundred million years, hoping, perhaps, that this, too, will pass. There are isolated populations above the dam in Holyoke and in the estuary below, and a modest breeding and study program is under way.

Of more immediate interest to those on the Connecticut, and especially anyone wishing to undertake any construction or alteration within the river itself, is the thoroughly unglamorous dwarf wedge mussel. This otherwise unprepossessing creature seems to have won the heart of one biologist, who can be counted on to show up when and wherever the mussel is discovered, snorkeling and scuba diving upstream and down, locating them at the foot of proposed bridge abutments, bank stabilization projects, and other riverine incursions. At first this is pretty scary to project managers and engineers, but the solution insisted upon, federal law in hand, is simply to move the mussels a short distance away. A day of mussel moving, especially if it is a hot summer day, can be a lot of fun, and there is a small team of professionals ready to do the work.

Compared to other endangered species, the dwarf wedge mussel is a cinch, and they're returning to their former range in droves. Part of the reason for this is better water quality. Like the rest of the forty or so species of freshwater clams and mussels in the Connecticut, they're filter feeders and particularly sensitive to the effects of pollution. But there may be another reason, too. Mussels are unique bivalves in that they require an intermediate host in the early stages of their life cycle. The minute larva of each mussel species must find a particular matching host species of fish, which it then parasitizes by forming small, harmless cysts in the gills. Only later will it drop free and drift to the bottom, where it will grow a shell and remain immobile. Of the fish species essential for the dwarf wedge mussel, one is the tessellated darter, a close relative of the snail darter, and the other is the immature Atlantic salmon.

The discovery of the life cycle of the dwarf wedge mussel, like the habitat of the snail darter and the technology of radio tracking, is part of a huge body of scientific knowledge that has only recently emerged. Just as the computer industry likes to point out that the speed and capacity of its machines is doubling every five years, so is humankind's overall body of knowledge. This may in fact be the greatest revolution of all, slowly driving a stake in the heart of the status quo. The number of scientists in the field, and the sophistication of their tools, has grown explosively, too, and this is partly, but by no means only, as a result of legislation and court decisions.

We have just recently begun to have access to this knowledge as a tool for long-term resource management, while long-term management is an anathema in today's climate of frontier capitalism. After four or five generations of being reared in the hatchery of consumerism, the public has little appetite for science anyway. Even global warming seems to have become yesterday's news. Whales, bald eagles, and Atlantic salmon remain market celebrities, and shortnose sturgeons get left behind. Unfortunately, the environmental movement itself thus also becomes more vulnerable. It undermines itself, and the great overarching vision of ecology, of science and information, is lost. Human sciences such as economics and medicine and sociology are part of our earth's ecology, too, and its health, and our health, are inextricably woven together.

On the fourteenth of July, five weeks after she had first been netted and tagged in Holyoke, fish number 42 was located. She was in a cool, shaded pool hardly larger than a bathtub, just twenty miles from the shopping malls of Brattleboro, high up in the hills of Ball Mountain Brook. There, in a run of clear, cold water so small one could cross it by stepping from stone to stone, she rested in the dappled shade, having completed her journey at last. Jay visited her whenever he could, parking his truck some distance away in case someone was watching. She stayed there through the long dry summer while the batteries inside her slowly ran down. She was there after Hurricane Floyd roared through, swelling her brook into a torrent, but she was gone by November, probably having mated with a stocked parr, gone to sea, or gone entirely.

Would you like to know what she looked like? Just go to the supermarket. They always have Atlantic salmon in the fish department, and often display them whole, body arched as though leaping. Note the slender, powerful build; the silvery sides with small, cruciform black dots. Imagine what it was like to see this sort of fish in a mountain pool, or see hundreds of them, if not thousands, leaping up the Connecticut. Some say that soon the imagination is all you will have left, for the farming of Atlantic salmon, which began in the early 1980s with such high hopes for saving the wild stocks, may now pose the greatest threat to the species of all.

Starting in Norway, then spreading to the Pacific Northwest and finally the Northeast, the aquaculture of Atlantic salmon was originally intended to take some of the commercial pressure off wild stocks. But just as is true of any other agricultural or manufacturing enterprise these days, the commercial success of a few inventive pioneers attracted the attention of the big marketers, who have taken over, driven the price down, and even developed what is referred to by some as the genetically modified "Frankenfish," which reaches market size in one-third the time. As with other genetically modified crops, the long-term effects on the environment that the escape of this new creation might have are simply ignored in the rush toward greater profits.

Modern salmon farms have been called floating pig farms, and it is an apt comparison in terms of both industrialization and pollution. After the young fish are started in freshwater hatcheries, they are transferred to floating pens in sheltered saltwater bays. They are fed pellets made out of industrially harvested sea fish. The pellets contain food coloring to make the flesh pink, along with alarming levels of contaminants such as PCBs. The copious amounts of uneaten food, feces, dead fish, and medications are themselves a significant form of pollution in these bays. The penned fish are often heavily parasitized, especially by sea lice, which hang from them in thready beards and will quickly attack and parasitize any native fish that should be so unlucky as to swim nearby.

Worse yet, the salmon are always escaping. A few manage to leap out all the time, but a great many are released during storms, to such an extent that now, in the commercial so-called wild fishery off Iceland, nearly half the fish caught are escapees from salmon farms, bringing their altered genetics and their diseases with them. The Atlantic salmon, which was for so long a symbol of the power and mystery of life, has now also become a symbol of corruption.

11

It's not that easy bein' green.
— Kermit the Frog

It is water's capacity as a solvent that makes it the giver of life. This elegant simplicity makes all of life's complexity possible. It is as true in a single cell of existence as it is the moment a river is born. The very first drops of rain contain the dissolved gases of the atmosphere and, upon falling, add the traces of minerals and organics that salmon can detect and retrace to the source. These gases and minerals are what in turn make metabolism possible, but they alone are not enough for the robust life of a river. Richer nutrients are needed, which can feed the microorganisms, which can in turn feed the higher forms of life, and trees are a major source of nutrients in most river systems.

The great riverside trees, growing tall in the fertile and moist alluvial soil, do more than shade the water and keep it cool, or create habitat when they fall in and are tumbled into the snags and jams and scour holes that characterize a truly wild river. They also supply a feast of leaves, which are quickly digested and converted into higher forms of life. The great logs and root masses themselves go more slowly, sometimes taking centuries to wend their way seaward and eventually disappear into the digestive tracts of various organisms, or the stygian morass. More nutrients wash in from the adjoining forest floor, rich with the sweet sugars of decomposition, but often this is still not quite enough.

In the relatively young rivers of the Northwest, which otherwise tend to be nutrient poor, it is the corpses of dead salmon that make up the deficit. In the great, heart-wrenching saga of the returning salmon, in which the heroic adults finally throw themselves onto the ultimate sacrificial altar of parenthood, they really do nourish the next generation. In the East the sea lamprey plays a similar role. It, too, stops feeding the moment it enters fresh waters from the sea and begins the long journey upstream, and it, too, dies after spawning. It is only when this maligned parasitic eel becomes inadvertently landlocked in freshwater lakes that it becomes a pest.

The corpses of fish are as rich a fertilizer to the river as they were to the riverside Indians planting their corn; the decaying bodies are joined by leaves and woody debris and the nutrients that wash in from our farm fields and barnyards today. But with all good things, it is also possible to get too much. The organisms of decomposition also use up the dissolved oxygen in the water. More oxygen may be put back in by the natural aeration of rapids and wind and rain, as well as the respiration of water plants, but if the nutrients are too rich, the water can become too low in oxygen to support aerobic life. The water body may even become saturated with toxic gases, such as hydrogen sulfide and methane. These conditions are usually only found in the depths of lakes, but they are more common in reservoirs where flooding has made nutrient levels higher anyway, and now in rivers where humans have added their own unique brew.

In just one century the widespread adoption of the indoor toilet and industrial processes such as washing and dyeing cloth and making paper turned the Connecticut into what was called "the most beautifully landscaped sewer in America." In many reaches the river was "dead" — anoxic and poisoned. The legacy of that age is still left behind in the sludge of the river's bed here and there, but for the most part the harm of the past century was mitigated within twenty years of the passage of the Clean Water Act. It is a public investment that has paid off at least a hundredfold even if one limits the benefits to the human species alone. River-based tourism and recreation have become a major industry, public health has benefited, and riverside real estate is at a premium instead of something to be avoided.

Traveling downstream, riverside towns that once turned their backs toward the river have discovered riverside parks. One is increasingly likely to encounter people out for an evening paddle, instead of an evening stroll, as the Connecticut swings lazily back and forth between farmland and tall riverside trees. Freed from the bounds of Fifteen Mile Falls, the river then resumes its southerly course, interrupted only briefly by lesser instream dams at Wilder and Bellows Falls, swelling with the waters of major tributaries — great Indian names that tumble like the waters themselves: the Passumpsic, the Ammonoosuc, the Ompompanoosuc; terse Anglo-Saxon names: the Waits, the Wells, the White. They bring the flavor of the hills, fifty villages, hundreds of farms with them in a rising seaward symphony.

Dozens of lesser brooks and streams enter, too, each

adding to the flow, and almost always, where a tributary enters the main stem, a broad fan of alluvial deposits spreads out like a miniature of the Nile or Mississippi Delta. Shaped like a hand, water running through the fingers, these flat, spreading deposits of sand, gravel, and fertile loam are one of the richest environments of the river. The channel often becomes braided, crossing and recrossing gravel bars, running between islands. The river itself becomes more dynamic, too, pushed against the opposite shore by the intruding water and sediments. More islands form from alluvial deposits downstream. Huge island trees, nurtured by rich soils and isolated from centuries of timber harvest, lean over the waters, draped with vines. Ferns grow six and eight feet tall. Rare plants and insects thrive, protected from agriculture. Waterfowl breed in the cutoff and stagnant sloughs left behind when the channels shift, as they always do, in the lifting and laying down.

A paddler going down the increasingly big-shouldered river is often unaware of what goes on beyond the immediate bank. A dense veil of trees and the high bank itself keep the illusion of wilderness. An interstate highway now runs alongside just off to the west, and riverside towns are getting larger, but often the only immediate sign of civilization is an increase in the number of old tires, some abandoned shopping carts, or an ominous pipe protruding from the bank and dribbling an opaque liquid. Another nutrient. The great alluvial fans, which are so inviting to the canoeist, are also where municipalities tend to build their sewage treatment plants.

Shit goes downhill, and towns tend to grow at the confluence of tributaries. These alluvial fans are the lowest place nearby, and generally this is land that is not valuable for more lofty real estate development. The impact is usually not as big as one might think, and certainly preferable to not treating the sewage at all. A combination of settling ponds, aerators, and agitators use various processes to remove "solids," the turds and toilet paper, and reduce the pathogens, generally well away from public view. Often the only hint of their presence is a rather fruity whiff of air, but you still don't want to spend much time near the water they put back in the river.

Most of these plants were built in the 1970s, largely with the federal funds made available with the Clean Water Act. They were designed according to a certain planned capacity — that is, the amount of present and future sewage they could handle, taking into account the municipality's projected growth over the next thirty years or so, plus any nearby industries and other demands such as the processing of added septage pumped from the tanks of homes beyond the sewer lines. The river's "assimilative capacity" is also taken into account. Natural dilution, aeration, and biotic activity in the river itself can work wonders within a few miles downstream of a treatment plant. An increase in the river's volume and flow means that it can handle more discharge.

Two problems were becoming increasingly apparent, however, as the hot dry summer of 1999 got under way. For one thing, most of these plants were nearing the end of their designed lifetime. This was especially a problem in midvalley areas, where growth and real estate development had been faster than anticipated. There had been upgrades here and there, but the federal funds that had once been so common were now nearly gone. As with the unfunded mandates of education, more and more of the financial burden was being placed on the municipalities alone. In addition, the assimilative capacity of the river itself was diminishing. The natural flows were down enough because of the drought, but this business of playing the spot market for electricity demand was making things a lot worse. There were places, and times, when the effluent from treatment plants was simply being discharged into stagnant pools, while the utility waited for the price to rise.

That Vice President Al Gore should decide to go canoeing at this place and time was a prophecy few heeded. But the isolation from reality that seems to characterize politics on both sides of the spectrum was happily at work, and the so-called environmental candidate was about to step in something so sticky and deep he would remain forever tainted.

The occasion was to be a celebration of the Connecticut's designation as an American Heritage River, and the ceremonial passing of a large foam-core check for $819,000 in federal funds to enhance the historic, environmental, and economic resources of the Connecticut River. These were funds that had already been allocated for river-related projects, American Heritage or not, but never mind. It would be more than a photo opportunity. Gore had just formally announced his candidacy for the presidency, and nearly every important person in government and environmental affairs in the region would be there, with two exceptions. One was me. Although our organization was a sponsor, and I was at the time president of the Vermont commission, I just couldn't bring myself to do it. I'd been on a lot of junkets, in canoes and on shore, and enjoyed most of them. But there was something creepy about this one.

The other exception was Governor Dean. During the previous winter he had traveled to Washington and confided to Gore that he might like to run for president someday. He hadn't even left the White House before Gore blurted this news to the waiting press, delivering a severe blow to both the governor's immediate political prospects and confidence in the White House itself. Loyal as we were to the

Connecticut, having by now canoed nearly the entire river's length together, we expressed our regrets. I would be haying, no matter what the weather would bring, and the governor would be at a greater remove, in Texas.

Gore's team conferred with the river commission. A scenic spot was chosen that would fit into his schedule of other stops that day — a stretch of river that included passage under the longest covered bridge in the world. The famous Cornish Colony lay among the hills on the eastern shore, and Mount Ascutney rose boldly to the west. A three-mile float by canoe would take just about an hour, allowing plenty of time to get the press corps, local dignitaries, and others into the canoes, even assuming that some of them had never been in a canoe before.

Two days before the trip some of Gore's staff, along with Secret Service agents and a team of navy SEALs, met commission staff for a run-through, and it became clear to them that the increasingly serious drought would pose some major problems. The SEALs, for example, were simply wading back and forth in their wet suits and diving gear, looking for explosives, one supposes, in water that was about eight inches deep. Rocks and gravel bars were exposed everywhere, and furthermore what water there was stank. Not only did the river not look good or smell good, but there were safety issues as well. People would keep running aground. The trip could take several hours instead of the one allotted.

The remedy seemed simple. PG&E could release some extra water from its dam upstream at Wilder. This was something it had done frequently in the past, to accommodate special trips or instream construction projects, something it was doing several times a day anyway; it would simply mean receiving a lower price for the electricity they would still be generating. A quick phone call cinched it: The dam operator would open the gates two hours earlier than usual on the day of the Gore trip.

Everything seemed to be going perfectly that day. The weather was sunny and warm, the river was about ten inches higher, and the vice president really didn't seem all that wooden after all, in his khaki slacks and polo shirt. He's no stranger to canoes, either, quite at home with a paddle on the water and the governor of New Hampshire in the bow, while some of the others fumbled and almost tipped over, or in some cases sat facing the wrong way. He said the right things, too: "We need to make the twenty-first century the time when we right the wrongs of our environmental past. We have to recognize our rivers for what they are: great national treasures that need to be protected."

There were three busloads of people on shore to hear his words; only a selected few got to actually go on the trip in the sixteen canoes provided, and seats were generally assigned randomly. Vermont's administration was represented by the Agency of Natural Resources secretary, and he wasn't sure just who it was in the bow of his canoe as they paddled southward with the flotilla. He may have been feeling a bit cranky, too; not everybody enjoys these things. Then at one point the man in the bow remarked that at least there was enough water, and the secretary replied; "Yeah, they'll release extra water for the vice president, but they won't release any for the salmon." Or words to that effect. It didn't really matter what the exact words were, because the man in the bow was a reporter for the *Washington Times*, and by nightfall he had fashioned the remark into "New Hampshire Able to Float Gore's Boat," the paper's top political story, an exposé on how the "environmental" candidate had squandered four billion gallons of water during a severe drought for a photo opportunity.

In today's media climate, in which stories are tossed upon

the waters in the hope of a feeding frenzy, it does not matter that the *Washington Times* is an ultraconservative newspaper run by the Moonie sect, or that it had nearly all of its facts wrong. Rush Limbaugh and Don Imus took the story and ran with it the next morning, playing it up in the anti-intellectual locker room of talk radio. By evening all the networks had piled on, and in the days that followed the *New York Times* called it a "mishap," the *Washington Post* ridiculed "four billion gallons for a photo op," and *Newsweek* called it "the photo op from hell." New Hampshire Republicans, who had been observing the Connecticut River Canoe Conspiracy all along, were quick to jump in, too. The Republican Party chairman held a press conference at a boat landing on the Merrimack, in Concord, and charged that Gore was a "pseudo-environmentalist" and that Pacific Gas and Electric had made what amounted to an illegal campaign contribution worth seven million dollars.

PG&E, the Connecticut River Joint Commissions, and many other official organizations quickly responded with their own press releases, pointing out, among many other errors, that the amount of water actually released was just a tenth of what had been reported, that the "price" of seven million dollars was apparently based on the cost of drinking water in Nashua, and that this was done all the time anyway. But the press turned a deaf ear, getting more mileage out of the story as originally reported, and formal complaints against PG&E were filed with the New Hampshire Attorney General, and by the Republican National Committee as well.

As usual, Republicans were running circles around Democrats. With the military speed and force that had evolved through years of fighting communism, they exploited this new opportunity as all others. It was like watching a match between Mister Rogers and Attila the Hun. The details they got wrong were irrelevant or, worse, boring. The "environmental candidate" was looking like a phony. And the Gore team should have seen it coming. They should have known that the American Heritage designation was political fluff to begin with. They should have been aware of water conditions and the downside of artificially manipulating a river's level, especially because almost the same thing had happened to Gore just three years before in Colorado, when there was a flap about jacking up the South Platte for a photo op.

If the event had been held on one of PG&E's reservoirs at Fifteen Mile Falls, if instead of canoes there had been motorboats and pretty girls on Jet Skis, perhaps Al Gore would be president today. But rather like an Atlantic salmon himself, Gore was in strange and hostile waters. The climate was changing, and we were loving it. The marbled blue planet was hardly more than a beach toy. He could talk the talk of the 1970s, but he couldn't walk the walk, didn't have the strength to fight the tepid tide of pollsters, marketing gurus, and media consultants. He didn't ask the right questions. He wasn't interested in what was really happening, on the river or off. He didn't have the balls.

It was somehow fitting that this happened here, within a few miles of where Vermont's own independence was first declared and constitution framed, and almost exactly halfway between the river's source and the sea. It was a turning point, a place to reflect on the past and speculate on what lay ahead. Here one begins to feel the river's great weight and destiny as it carries us.

In 1777, the year that Vermont proclaimed its independence, there were salmon naturally spawning in the river here.

Adam Smith had published *An Inquiry into the Nature and Causes of the Wealth of Nations* just the year before, mainly as a treatise against inept meddling with the economy by King George. Bloodletting was state-of-the art medicine. The term *corporation* was virtually unknown beyond the original colonial charters; it was mainly a legal umbrella for charities. A lot of people still had trouble accepting the theories of Copernicus.

The constitution of the Republic of Vermont was the first to outlaw slavery. It was the first to extend the right to vote beyond those who owned land. It was the first to legislate an education for all citizens at public cost. A little more than two centuries later, in September 1998, my hometown hosted a conference: "Should the Government Control Our Forests?" The conference was in response to the Northern Forest Stewardship Act, an act passed because of the precipitous "liquidation" of the northern forest of New York, Vermont, New Hampshire, and Maine by multinational corporations. The act called for federal funding to study the situation, nothing more, but the property rights activists insisted that it was part of a government takeover, and their inflammatory words sounded like the sort of revolution our forefathers would have agreed with. Except that control would therefore be even more firmly in the hands of corporations and at a farther remove from a democratic society.

The list of conference sponsors seemed impressive; the Associated Industries of Vermont, the Alliance for America, the American Land Rights Association, the BlueRibbon Coalition, Georgia-Pacific Corporation, the Vermont Farm Bureau, and the Vermont Forest Products Association were among them. The list of speakers was more impressive still, leading off with Ron Arnold of the Center for the Defense of Free Enterprise. He was followed by Chuck "rent-a-riot"

Cushman, who sees the National Park Service, the USDA Forest Service, and the U.S. Fish and Wildlife Service plotting together to make the forest "part of a vast wilderness playground, where private property will be appropriated for wildlife through land use restrictions."

But despite the best efforts of the organizers and the local newspaper, turnout for the conference was low. The memory of Carl Drega's shooting rampage was still too fresh. The speakers and sponsors almost outnumbered the attendees. Only about seventy tickets were sold, and Arnold, Cushman, and the others returned to their rapt audiences in Idaho, Montana, and the Pacific Northwest.

12

In America today you can murder the land for private profit. You can leave the corpse for all to see, and nobody calls the cops.

— Paul Brooks

Night by the river, embraced by the valley, going to sleep with stars in my eyes. A church bell tolls the hour in a nearby riverside town, calling for peace, for order and tranquility. A pause, then the coyotes make their wild, chaotic reply, thrilling as the stars themselves. Then sleep comes, as silken as the river itself slipping by, unbroken until a flock of Canada geese takes flight at first light and wheels low overhead. They nest here now, in greater numbers every year. Stir the coals in the big old log. Add some cedar for its scented smoke, an offering to the day. Cows are gathering for their milking at the hillside barn, their calls a baritone counterpoint to the birds, and for some reason a woodchuck has decided to swim the river, coming toward me plowing a V-shaped wake through the still, misty waters. It comes right to the campsite, past my fire without looking at me, and continues up into the fields in a perfectly straight line.

The river valley is awakening with the hum of machinery:

milking machines, automobiles. The din of civilization gets louder. We are off and under way by the time the big machines come out, diesel tractors spreading manure and mowing what grass there is this year. The raw sweet smells of the work come in waves on the rising breeze. Later, when the dew is off and the sun is nearly overhead and the grass cut yesterday is worked, there is the rich, tea-like smell of curing hay, the best smell of all. I home in on it, like a salmon myself, inescapably drawn. It was the magic of agriculture that set our minds free, just as the magic of fire drew us down from the trees. I walk among farmers as among giants. If "their way of life is finished anyway," as is said of the Northern Cree, then mine is, too, and so is yours. No more communion of body and spirit, no more church bells and coyotes.

Farmers, when they meet at the few tractor dealerships and feed stores that are left, talk about the weather as they have for ten thousand years. "Dry, isn't it?" They stomp about and scowl at prices and squint at the sun. Under the burning sun and the great wheeling of the days of that dry year of '99, the drought was occasionally broken by floods. There were weeks, almost months when just a few drops of rain would fall, exploding like bombs in the dust — actually sending up little clouds of it — and small streams would dry up entirely during the day, only to return at night, shyly creeping out of the woods when the transpiration of trees had stopped. Farmers grimly spoke of the Dust Bowl days, when everything seemed to go wrong at once, even though it was in their grandfathers' time, not their own. All around the world this was happening, not just in Vermont. Then the floods would come, sweeping in from the Atlantic, or the Indian Ocean, or the South China Sea. There was talk of global warming, but less such talk here than abroad, as the wind blew more steadily from the right.

Meanwhile, somewhere within the rabbit warren of offices of the Vermont Agency of Natural Resources, enclosed by the grim institutional brick walls of what was once the state insane asylum, a researcher decided to revisit the data on mercury in fish tissue that had been gathered during the Fifteen Mile Falls relicensing process. The tissues of various types and age classes of fish in the three reservoirs had been analyzed for mercury content as just one of the dozens of studies the settlement had required. As with the other studies, the job had been contracted out to a consulting firm with experience in the field. The fish had been collected, the tissue was examined in a laboratory, and the results were then submitted to the New Hampshire Department of Environmental Services for review.

As originally analyzed, there didn't seem to be anything alarming about the data, which is important, because where excessive mercury in fish tissues has been reported elsewhere it has had severe consequences for both wildlife and humans that eat the fish. The effect of chronic exposure to mercury is named Minamata disease, for the seaside town in Japan where perhaps hundreds died and many thousands were affected by eating fish contaminated with mercury. The symptoms include nervous disorders and reproductive problems, and very high levels of mercury had been detected in fish tissues elsewhere in New England, especially in reservoirs where the water levels were subject to severe fluctuations.

The Vermont researcher discovered that the data had been misinterpreted. The levels of mercury in the fish of Fifteen Mile Falls were in fact two to almost three times those of fish from adjacent water bodies, and well beyond the threshold requiring a consumption advisory to the public. When this news was shared with New Hampshire the appropriate advisories were promptly issued, limiting consumption of fish especially among children and pregnant women, just as they had been for the Cree of northern Quebec, and a series of confrontational meetings were convened between parties of the relicensing settlement and representatives of Pacific Gas and Electric.

The executives of PG&E's New England hydrogeneration facilities had, by this time, forsaken the modest, drab cubicles of New England Power, which had been in a corner of a large utility vehicle maintenance garage. Now the executives had plush offices in a brand-new business park a few miles up the road. In the blink of an eye they had gone from instant coffee to café latte. For the most part the same familiar faces were there, but the faces seemed to be smiling a lot more, though not necessarily at us, and there were some nice new cars in the lot, too.

As negotiators, we got to use the conference room and sit in swivel chairs, facing each other over the polished wood of the classic lozenge-shaped conference table. Speakerphones, computers, and audiovisual equipment lay at hand. At first there was a lot of swiveling, but then we got down to business. The license was very important to the utility, and it didn't see the mercury as a deal breaker. Predictably, its response was to deny any responsibility. We said it was responsible, and the license could be delayed. The company representatives said mercury is everywhere, and they're right, but lately it seems to be emerging as an insidious poison that reflects our extravagant lifestyle.

This rather rare and intriguing metal, which schoolchildren used to play with and which is commonly used to fill our teeth, is relatively inert in its pure form. It's naturally present in varying amounts in soils and can be a waste product of industrial processes, as was the case in Minamata. Now, however, it is increasingly coming from the air — from the burning of fossil fuels, trash incinerators, and even, to a small but gruesome extent, crematoriums. Explorations of soil profiles show that the deposition of mercury from the air has increased dramatically in the past twenty years in concert with the increased use of coal for electrical power generation.

Still, though, mercury as such doesn't become the very deadly poison it is until it becomes methylated, that is, combines with organic compounds that make it water soluble. Bacterial activity methylates mercury. It is more likely to happen in soils that have a high humus content, especially the deep rich alluvial soils of river valleys. This is an anaerobic process that takes place in water, and the process is accelerated when these soils are subjected to fluctuating water levels. The water containing methylated mercury is squeezed out as the water level drops, and the process resumes when the soil is flooded again. The methylmercury is first ingested by the lowest members of the food chain, the zooplankton, and then ascends through small fish to larger fish and fish eaters such as loons, kingfishers, and humans. Because it is excreted only at a very slow rate, it becomes more concentrated as one ascends the food chain, to the point where it is documented to affect the breeding success of wildlife and puts humans at risk.

But just as tobacco companies have long argued that there is no proof that cigarettes cause lung cancer, the utilities, too, deny a causal relationship even though the evidence is strongly against them. Pacific Gas and Electric sort of went halfway, saying that if indeed most mercury pollution today does come from coal-burning power plants, then hydrogeneration is a preferable alternative. It contested the data asserting that reservoirs with fluctuating water levels made the problem worse. The debate between lawyers and biologists on both sides went back and forth for a year before the utility agreed to monitor mercury through the license term and con-

tribute half a million dollars to a mercury mitigation program, which mainly consists of removing mercury from the
waste stream.

Our organization encouraged taking a closer look at what
else might be in the river, and assisted the EPA in a sediment
sample study in the river's upper reaches. Nobody had ever
done this before, and mercury, as just one example, used to
be a by-product of certain papermaking processes. A sediment core sample was to be taken in any likely reach —
wherever the current slowed and fine material was deposited,
especially below alluvial fans, industrial areas, and municipalities, as well as behind impoundments. We began enthusiastically planning the fieldwork, consulting local residents in
the selection of the sampling sites. During one of our local
planning sessions, a representative from the consulting firm
that would be doing the work happened to casually mention
that its protocol required its technicians to wear Tyvek suits
with rubber boots and gloves while doing the work.

Suddenly what had seemed like it might be both fun and
instructive began to look ridiculous as well. Many of the residents of the Upper Valley were still convinced that the Silvio
Conte Wildlife Refuge was part of a plot by the United
Nations, and there were already rumors of men in chemical
warfare suits being spotted at night, especially as the millennium drew closer. We asked why on earth anyone would
want to wear a hot, sticky Tyvek suit to take samples from a
river in which the rest of us cavorted wearing swimsuits or
less, and they answered in humorless monotone that it wasn't
just the river, it was the possibility of ticks and poison ivy on
the shorelines, too.

What a weird society we have come to live in. Perhaps it is

the constant threat of litigation that has made us all so defensive. Certainly it is in the interest of the makers of Tyvek to encourage people to wear one of their suits at all times. But it is more than an affront to me personally, as one who believes in both science and common sense, and proposes that they may in fact be the same thing. This was the same exploitation of fear and anxiety that advertisers use to sell bug zappers and household disinfectants. Talk about loss of vision! In the Byzantine and bureaucratic halls of an environmental consulting firm, the environment itself had become an adversary.

It took a lot of convincing, besides the assertion that somebody in a Tyvek suit might get shot, to get them to just take the samples wearing plain clothes, which they finally did. And this is what they found. In most places there were the usual contaminants: some hydrocarbons here, a little DDT there, some heavy metals downstream of former industries, a lot of copper downstream from a former copper mine. There was nothing extraordinary, nothing unexpected, until they got all the way up to that beaver pond high in the headwaters where both the river and this book begins. There, in the black muck at the bottom of that serene pool, they found mercury, lots and lots of mercury. It was off the chart, ten times what was found anywhere else.

Conjecture is that this is at least in part because of the pond's location, near the height of land on a great divide. Just as is the case with acid rain, these high mountain ridges are the first to intercept polluted air that has traveled a great distance. This is why so many trees are dying, especially red spruce, at high elevations more than anywhere else. But there is something symbolic, too, about this poison in our headwaters, in this place that still seems so much like our frontier. That which we have taken to be most pure, we have fundamentally tainted.

And yet as long as the mercury stays in sediments, it isn't particularly harmful. The next question was whether it was indeed staying there, so we undertook a second study with folks from the EPA to sample fish tissues. Then two really ominous things happened. The first was that they ran out of money before reaching the headwaters. They never got any fish samples up there. The second was that the lab lost the data from the other samples they had managed to get. This sort of thing has happened before, and seems to be happening a lot more lately. This particular matter has gone to court, and resides there still as I write. Sooner or later someone will force a closer look at mercury and the other contaminants in fish tissue upstream of Fifteen Mile Falls, but it will likely be later because funding for this sort of thing is drying up fast, and the implications, if the fish are unsafe to eat, are enormous. It will mean there is a violation of the Clean Water Act, and it could open the doors for legal actions against midwestern utilities, although there is also an effort under way in Congress to rewrite the Clean Water Act so that places such as the headwaters of the Connecticut will no longer be included.

Behold a government that has become totally enfeebled and confused by itself; an international pariah, in denial about global warming, and obsessed with meaningless distractions like West Nile virus. Long ago, when spring came to the hill farms where I live and the roads finally dried out, the legendary Yankee peddlers would wend their way northward with their carts of patent medicines, kitchenwares, and sewing supplies. Like anyone else who came up the lane, lurching over the ruts and trailing a plume of dust when the season got dry, they could be seen from a long way off; they were something to watch for from the shade of the front porch. The family tended to leave their chores and gather to hear their pitch, at once amused and skeptical. The peddlers were quick with a joke or a snippet of news or gossip, not to be trusted entirely for they brought city ways with them, too, but it was a form of entertainment for the upland families as well as a way of keeping in touch with modern times.

Who back then could have imagined that just over a hundred years later, the farmers would nearly all be gone, and the hucksters would have taken over almost entirely? Impressed as I had been by the efforts of the Northern Cree to keep their identity, keep their spiritual and cultural connections, I am also still haunted by the image of my host up there who was addicted to the endomorphic opera of the World Wrestling Federation. We seem to be following the same course he chose for himself, forsaking each other in the name of self-centered survival "reality," forsaking the mysteries of life for evangelical pulp fiction. On the television, the advertisements show a new relationship with the environment, one that requires Tyvek but also one with New Age permissiveness and a quasi-religious air in which the mountains and prairies and wetlands are a playpen for people with power and a personal covenant with the creator. In this rootless place, where families move every few years to another place that looks just the same, the marketers, the peddlers, the hucksters, in their ascendance, not only have destroyed our culture, but are in the process of destroying our democracy as well, creating instead a dictatorship designed for spoiled children, fueled by sound bites and driven by the promise of instant gratification.

13

The body politic, like the human body, begins to die from birth, and bears it itself the causes of its own destruction.

— Jean-Jacques Rousseau

Our trip down the Connecticut River with Howard Dean and his family took years, doing just two or three days at a time in summer when time permitted, and going back to repeat some of our favorite segments. We began the source-to-sea trip on a May morning as high up on Indian Stream as we could get. There was still snow and ice along the banks. We often had to jump out into the icy water and drag the canoes. Our children, then on the cusp of adolescence, hung over the bows pointing out rocks. By the time we made our last trip our oldest children were preparing for college. Howard was in his fifth two-year term, and he had his eye on the presidency.

Howard had continued to practice medicine after he entered politics, first as a legislator and then as lieutenant governor. It was a profession he loved and was very good at, but one that he gave up after the previous governor, a staunch conservative, unexpectedly died in office. For a few years after that, he thought he might go back to medicine again, but he was also aware that modern medicine demands constant practice simply in order to remain fit for it. Gradually political leadership became the consuming challenge and he practiced this, too, as a physician would, often blunt and impolitic himself, but remaining focused on the health of a society.

He maintained his predecessor's conservative fiscal policies, but he was challenged by the professional politicians, who tend to be lawyers, from the start. He hated gambling, for example, and saw state lotteries as unhealthy for the human spirit, destructive of the ethic of labor and reward. This won him enemies on both sides of the legislature, as did his balanced approach to both business interests and the environment, which he tended to treat holistically, as a physician would, with the long-term risks and benefits in mind. He recognized that a nation's greatest resource is not its oil, its coal or minerals, or its trees, water, and soil. A nations's greatest resource is its people, and they can be mined and exploited for only so long. Health care, education, and security are what keep a nation healthy and growing.

His popular support grew all the while, but his opponents were as fervent as his supporters, and the week's political events would often continue to resonate through our discussions on our canoeing weekends. Early on, many Vermonters had complained about the massive clear-cuts of timber that were taking place, particularly in the state's headwaters region, as the timber companies liquidated their assets and pulled out, one after another. Vermont didn't have any legislation regulating clear-cuts. Most other states did by then. The legislature passed a bill calling for an approved forestry plan for any clear-cut of more than forty acres. It was a reasonable measure in response to public outcry, but the outcry was louder from the loggers and truckers once the property rights activists got them up in arms, figuratively if not literally. Log trucks were disrupting appearances by the governor, honking their horns or using their Jake Brakes to send big "raspberries" echoing above the crowd. He was reelected by a wide majority nonetheless.

Occasionally we combined politics with a canoe trip and invited local selectmen and legislators to join us. Howard listened to them as a physician would. Members of the press were invited more than once, too, but they declined, preferring to observe the canoe conspiracy from the shore. After the passage of the civil unions bill, which was the first in the nation to give legal status to gay couples, the opposition grew particularly hateful. As both the election and the deer-hunting season once again grew near, one bit of graffiti stands out in my memory above all others: REMEMBER IN NOVEMBER. SHOOT A QUEER, SAVE A DEER. Again, he was reelected by a wide margin.

State troopers had accompanied us on our trips. Originally it was as much for companionship as anything else — they often had their wives and kids along, too — but after the Drega shootings and all the threats that followed the clear-cutting and civil unions bills, the troopers were packing heat along with sandwiches and sleeping gear. Often I would scout our route a day or two ahead of time with one of the troopers, and over the years I became good friends with them, especially with Dennis, who was the lieutenant in charge of the governor's security detail. Among other things, he showed me some fishing techniques that I value highly to this day.

It was also the first time since my service in Vietnam that I had spent any time with other men who had chosen to serve their nation in uniform, and one of the few times since then that I'd felt free to talk about that experience, which they understood completely in terms of service and sacrifice, but not in terms of betrayal. This was not an experience that Howard had shared himself, either, but he still wore the belt that had belonged to his brother, who, as a young civilian adventurer, had been captured and then presumably executed by the Pathet Lao during the war. His loss remained as a deep, unhealed wound, another thing that we talked about by the fire, while watching the great river slip past and the tree line brooding on the far shore, not unlike the Mekong itself.

It was during those years, and at those times on the river, that I began to feel my own leadership once again, often with help from Howard, such as with his appointing me to the river commission. We accomplished a lot as a result. But my relationship with uniformed service, and with the law, has had its ups and downs over the years, and toward the end of our journey I was in a down phase, on the verge of being busted. I had been leading two lives: one as a respected citizen and one as a fugitive, part public servant and part perp. I kept up appearances for the public, but at home I was harboring a contraband bunny. I considered confiding to Howard and Dennis about it around the fire one night, but in the end decided against it. If I was going down, I didn't want to take them with me.

Nearly all my life I've been taking in wild animals with varying success, and over the years a small group of friends and underground veterinarians have assisted me, bringing me wild creatures and helping me bring them up for eventual release into the wild again. I was unaware until fairly recently that this sort of rehabilitation is illegal without a license, and that a license is virtually impossible to get in Vermont. I tried a dozen times to go straight, to quit for good, only to be tempted once again.

This time it was a snowshoe hare that, from the age of about twelve hours, had clearly imprinted on me. I carried Bunny in my front shirt pocket and fed her with an eyedropper, for she could easily sit in a tablespoon. In gratitude, she would lick my nose and nibble my eyebrows. I began to realize that unlike the foxes, skunks, raccoons, and other creatures I'd raised in the past, this bunny would not last more than five minutes in the wild. Besides, it would be an interesting experiment to keep her around. I wanted to see if she would still get the proper cues to turn white in winter. I wanted to see if it was really true that bunnies dance on their hind legs in the moonlight when they think nobody is watching.

So I called the local game warden (now retired) and left a recorded message of confession, hoping for some amnesty in return for a bunny permit. He returned my call when I was away, and treated my wife, who answered the call, as though he had just caught her with a dozen dead eagles in the trunk of her car, in tones some may call firm and others threatening. When I got home she was still in tears. We were on edge for months afterward, afraid every car that rumbled down the drive might be a SWAT team, but they never came. I suppose they were afraid it would turn into another Ruby Ridge or Montana Militia standoff, for I was angry enough by then to have put the word out through various channels that "they could have my bunny when they pry her from my cold, dead hand."

I realized that, given the circumstances, I was not entirely fit for public life, and that no matter how much I enjoyed the company of state troopers, we were fundamentally different. I find nuance where they tend to see black and white, and this will continue to get me in trouble. I also gradually figured out why the Vermont Fish and Wildlife Department despises bunny lovers. It is because the department depends on the income from hunting licenses for its funds. Few things are more ridiculed and reviled by its members than the "Bambi" syndrome. To suggest that bunnies, or that game animals in general, are anything more than sporting targets is extremely subversive to this authoritarian bureaucracy, especially now that there are fewer new hunters every year. Bunnies, too, are a regulated commodity.

On one of our last mornings, enveloped in the late-summer mist of dawn, the river was for once silent and serene. Tendrils of mist feathered upward from the warm water into the cool air. We were deep down in Massachusetts, but there were hardly any traffic sounds at all, just crows somewhere above the mist. We had taken a beating from the motorboats the day before, shipped a lot of water, and as we prepared breakfast I noticed that Howard was trying to use a box of Bisquick that had seen better days. It was battered and soaked with bilgewater. The cardboard carton was about to fall apart, and he was having a hard time finding dry mix inside. I offered a fresh new box, but he insisted on finishing the old one. Soggy though it was, he couldn't bear to waste it. What an anachronism, especially down here in the land of plenty, but also more evidence that he was the right man for political leadership, as obsessed with waste as he was with social health.

Then we were on the river again as the morning sun burned through and the mist billowed white against blue sky. We settled in, feeling the bob of the river beneath us. Lines of trees ahead slowly parted like curtains, revealing the next turn. The spruce and fir of the headwater boreal forest lay far behind us; we had traversed four climate zones, and now white oak and hickory mixed with the red oak and maple on the deep, rich soil of the river's banks. Here and there great domes of red Triassic sandstone rose above the surrounding land, breaking a broad floodplain. More red rock shouldered into the river between bright sand beaches where the power-boats had landed and set up camp, and boom-box music resounded from the riverbanks. When we camped at night, seeking more privacy and the permission of riverside landowners, we heard the constant rain of nuts falling down through the leaves and thudding on the forest floor. Such is the natural richness of this place, which was once known as the breadbasket of New England. In the thick riverine forest, where nut trees grew in alluvial soils as deep as those soils of the Mississippi Delta, it even rained bread at night.

There was still corn growing in the rich farmland that lay between shopping malls and suburban sprawls, but by the time we got near Northfield most of the nonpoint pollution — all the stuff that doesn't dribble into the river from a pipe — came from urban runoff and the pesticides used on golf courses and lawns, not farm fields. Every rainfall added a chemical soup flowing off the highways and parking lots, carrying all sorts of human, animal, and mechanical exudate that avoided treatment entirely, was unfiltered by soil, and went right into the great, warming, tiring river, which was farting and gasping on the last reaches toward the sea. We had watched the river's clarity steadily decline as we went down it, using our paddles as Secchi dishes. It would get murky below urban areas or where there were a lot of power-boats, and then slowly recover again, but now it wasn't recovering at all.

We had chosen a Labor Day weekend, and the water churned with the wakes of motorboats and Jet Skis. Rivers weren't built for this. Their banks don't have the natural armor against wave action, such as the vegetation, gravel, and stones that lakes have evolved. The soft mud riverbanks are insulted by wave after wave, and it is easy to watch the color of the water change through the day from clear to murky brown. The hotter and drier the summer, the lower the banks are, the more exposed mud there is, and the more the boats come, like angry hornets, spewing noise and oil and smoke to the applause of their manufacturers. This is not merely a matter of aesthetics. The murky water adds nutrients that use up oxygen, and it blocks off the sunlight to aquatic vegetation.

And yet there is a constant clamor in the state legislatures for even more motorized access to the river, access that doesn't "discriminate" against the powerboat crowd, and woe unto the group or organization that attempts opposition. In the broad lower reaches of the river, the boat wakes were more dangerous than any of the rapids we had run upstream. It was like riding a camel in the midst of Operation Desert Storm. And this was where the electricity generated by Fifteen Mile Falls went. This was where real estate interests were protected by those flood control dams in the headwaters.

It's not so much the loss of salmon, or the proliferation of the "generalists" that have adapted themselves to the filthy habits of humans — the carp and the pigeon, the cockroach and rat — that worries me. It's not just that the murky water and siltation suffocate all sorts of plant and animal life, or even the loud arrogance that makes it almost impossible for anyone without a motor to enjoy the river. It's the parching thirst for more oil itself and the bellicose disregard for fellow humans that are more compelling. It's that guy in the Humvee with a trailer hitch and a pair of Jet Skis towed behind that I'm really scared of.

Above the city of Holyoke, where the industrial age of the river began, and which today, from the river, appears to be a city in ruins, we decided to go ashore and rest for a while. We had been fighting the powerboats and headwinds all day, picking our way along the shore through the branches of overhanging trees. It was both hard work and depressing, and we needed a break. There was a good little beach behind a slant of red rock, and we put ashore, stretched our legs, and fumbled about for snacks.

There was a Puerto Rican family picnicking nearby; mother, father, and son of about twelve. The boy approached us shyly; there was a uniformed officer from the Massachusetts Environmental Police with us, and the kid was both curious and intimidated. But after a friendly exchange he relaxed and then asked us if we would like to see the dinosaur footprints. We sure did, so he led us up a footpath through the brush and bottles and cans and wrappers. This was a proud kid. He was happy to be there beside a river where he had a sense of ownership. He led us to where a slate ledge slanted out just below the highway. And there were the dinosaur tracks. No doubt about it. It looked like a flock of giant chickens, only with wider toes, had run across the ledge. And so they had, a hundred million years ago.

There we were, standing there ourselves, looking out across the river through the scraggly oaks toward the auburn sky. So much lay behind us, and so much ahead. If you would like to see what it was like here a hundred million years ago, you could try looking into the eye of a sturgeon. Looking ahead is more difficult, but scientists are now telling us of many more things in the river that we should know about; it isn't just our pesticides, our solvents, and what's left of our feces. Just look at the ingredients on a bottle of shampoo the next time you take a shower. Then add some chlorine, famously carcinogenic when it combines with organic compounds.

And the same chemicals that are in our blood are in the river, too. Our bodies, and the body of the river, are linked together in ways that are both mystical and ominous. There are heavy metals and DDT and PCBs in us as well as in the river, along with the ingredients of plastics, and flame retardants and pesticides. And in the river we are finding the medications we administer to ourselves and our livestock: the antibiotics and birth control pills and heart medications and steroids. Often as little as 1 percent of our medications is actually absorbed by our bodies. The rest goes in the river virtually unaltered, to be shared with everything else that lives there in what amounts to a huge biochemical experiment. Caffeine is ubiquitous, and some researchers report fish on Prozac.

Among the many effects observed in fish is one of "feminization." Fish are especially being affected by the imitators of estrogen that come from both our medications and the family of nonylphenols in detergents. The proportion of female fish in affected rivers rises dramatically. Male sex organs atrophy. Reproduction begins to drop off or fail completely. This is even observed in carp, one of the great generalist species that can survive almost anywhere, as well as the more sensitive species, where those species survive at all. And when salmon "smoltify" — that is, when they undergo the hormonal changes triggered by the length of the day and water temperature — they have only a brief window of opportunity, a hormonal clock ticking inside them so that they will be able to keep the right balance of electrolytes as they travel from the fresh water they were born in to the salty sea. If those smolt are delayed by, say, a reservoir, or if the balance of hormones is upset, the window closes. It may be that the salmon stocked at such great expense are hardly reaching the sea at all, that they are going belly-up somewhere in the estuary, desiccated by salt, as has been suggested by research in Canada.

But there is more. Now the bacteria that thrive in the nutrient-rich water and black muck of the river have become resistant to antibiotics. This is true in agricultural regions as well as urban ones, because livestock are heavily dosed with antibiotics so that they can tolerate the crowded and dirty conditions of big modern farms. Then waterfowl spread the resistant strains back to the land again, but what takes place next in the water may be more ominous still, for by sending our filth into the river and thence to the sea, we are by no means getting rid of it. The deep ocean acts as a sort of refrigerator, preserving pathogens rather than killing them.

All this may be fine, too, if — as with the mercury in the headwaters or other contaminants in sediments everywhere — everything remains immobile. But as the planet warms, as it surely is, there is increasing evidence of a great overturning beginning to taking place in the oceans, just as takes place in temperate-zone lakes when the water warms with springtime. In these lakes, as the surface ice melts and temperature gradient shifts, there comes a moment when suddenly the deep waters come upwelling to the surface, bringing a bonanza of nutrients with them. Should this happen in the oceans, the upwelling can bring more than nutrients; this may already be occurring in places such as coastal Bangladesh and Peru, where sudden oceanic plankton blooms have been accompanied by outbreaks of resistant cholera. It is possible, in fact, that as the planet warms and the oceanic currents change, there may be a sort of great global vomiting, in which it all comes up again, almost all at once — not just the pathogens and pollutants, but even the deadly methane that has lain there for so many millions of years, as though our planet has suddenly decided that it has had enough of us.

Real environmentalism is, by definition, inclusive. It includes the human, the social, and the economic environment. It does not see humankind as a separate entity, apart from the rules of nature. It recognizes the oneness of our own circulatory system with that of the river. It places consideration before exploitation. It relies on knowledge rather than emotion. It finds its roots in our democracy, and suggests the commonalities of both science and religion. And as such, real environmentalism is a revolutionary concept.

Meanwhile, as we neared the sea, I decided that I'd had enough of that particular part of the planet. I couldn't keep going downstream with Howard any longer. It had become too much a matter of physical endurance and inner reward for him, with little pleasure for me. I longed for the clear brooks of my home. I missed my bunny. I bailed out of the river trip near Springfield. But Howard kept going alone, bucking the increasing headwinds, buffeted by the wakes of ever-larger vessels: seagoing yachts and tugboats and oil barges. He kept going past Hartford, past Middletown and Wethersfield, bucking the tides themselves, totally focused. He exhausted even the state troopers, who ended up following him from the highway with binoculars as he fought his way like some sort of grim and determined salmon, and he finally reached his goal.

14

For all at last returns to the sea — to Oceanus, the
ocean river, like the ever-flowing stream of time, the
beginning, and the end.

— Rachel Carson,
The Sea Around Us

The next year, the year of the new millennium, the wettest
April on record was followed by an almost equally wet May.
Day after day, stubborn low-pressure systems remained
parked over northern Quebec, as though the Cree themselves
had placed a curse on us. Wave after wave of storm lines pin-
wheeled from the lows and swept across northern New
England; one moment the skies would be crystal clear, then
the lines of towering cumulus would come hurtling out of the
northwest again, bringing hail, high winds, and even a few
tornadoes along with the drenching rains. Many farmers gave
up trying to get their corn planted; where they did succeed,
the newly planted fields soon had standing water in them as
the soil became saturated.

Then the rains intensified, in a pattern that has become
increasingly common in the past twenty years, with prolonged
drought alternating with floods. The distribution of rainfall
varied widely; in some places there was little flooding, and in

others as much as six inches of rain fell in six hours. Unlike the rains of Hurricane Floyd the previous year, which had fallen upon parched soils, this time the earth could absorb no more. High in the forested hills, the rains swept through the canopy, dripped from the leaves, and streamed down the sides of trees. In the open, shattered debris of the clear-cuts, it gathered much more quickly, filling the skidder ruts, turning them into streams. Rivulets began their meander toward the sea, carrying a bit of bark here, a crumb of soil there, converging, carrying more. They moved at a walking pace at first. Then they began to move at a run. In some places the rain and subsequent runoff quickly exceeded anything that had been recorded, exceeded even the theoretical one-in-five-hundred-years flood. Beaver dams began to collapse like watershed dominoes, adding enormous pulses of floodwater to mountain streams, which then set about recarving their valleys.

Roads, which almost always follow streams, and which had gradually encroached upon the streams as the roads were improved and widened over the years, were the next to go, starting with the small-town dirt roads that wander up the narrow hollows. Uprooted trees fetched up on culverts and bridge abutments and caught more debris. The road itself briefly became a dam and a lake of brown water formed, pushing back into the woods. Then the road would all wash out in a rush of water and gravel, leaving guardrails dangling above the surging brown tide. In other places, at curves and narrows, the torrents would gradually eat into roadside embankments. Rolling boulders added their tympany to the roar. The only comparison, in terms of so much land being rearranged in such a hurry, might be a volcano.

Down in the broader valleys, huge alluvial fans of gravel spread out like lava fields under the flow. The water slowed and filled the floodplains where the low-cost housing lies, first filling the basements, then rising above the steps, creeping across the floors and up the walls. The National Guard was called out. Helicopters fluttered overhead, and boats cruised the main streets of upland towns. When the television newspeople thrust microphones at the wet and miserable faces of homeowners, they pleaded with the government to "do something" while mobile homes, propane tanks, and automobiles floated past in the background. In the newspaper, over the days that followed, some blamed the government itself, and the environmentalists who had recently passed laws regulating the commercial mining of gravel from streambeds. They said the rivers were flooding because there was too much gravel.

Pacific Gas and Electric claimed to be caught completely by surprise by the floods. The four lakes that the company maintains up in the headwaters are supposed to be for flood control as well as holding a reserve for generating electricity downstream during low-water months. But according to local residents the lakes were already full — no room had been allowed for more rain should it fall — so the surge carried right over the dams and on downstream, where the river came up so fast that some farmers were unable to retrieve their tractors from riverside fields, and others lost cattle to drowning.

Meanwhile, down at Fifteen Mile Falls itself, another smolt migration study was already under way, since the first one had turned out so poorly. This time 148 radio-tagged and fully "smoltified" smolts had been placed in the reservoirs. The humorless study reports that of the 108 smolts put in the head end of Moore Reservoir, 9 passed over the top of the dam. There was a 159-foot-high waterfall plunging over Moore Dam, and they plunged with it. It was the first time that water had passed over the top of that dam since it had been built in the 1950s. Somehow a tenth smolt got sucked into the turbine intake forty feet below the surface, and went through that.

Forty more smolt had been put into Comerford Reservoir, right at the foot of Moore before the flood. They stayed there. But four of the fish from Moore seemed to be on some sort of survivor high and went over the top of Comerford Dam, too, dropping 179 vertical feet this time. They actually seemed to be enjoying it, riding the crest of the flood like wired little surfers, which in fact they were. Three of them even showed up at Turners Falls, 167 miles downstream, a week later, still riding the crest and having passed through or over five more hydroelectric dams.

Although the biologists with the consulting firm that had been hired to perform the study said it was unlikely that any smolt would have made it through the reservoirs without the flood, the Vermont biologist commenting on the study said it was "heartening" to see this success, and as of this writing Pacific Gas and Electric has been asked by the U.S. Fish and Wildlife Service to come up with a plan that would duplicate the flood on a smaller scale every year by spilling water through the dams continuously during the smolt migration season, a sort of giant water slide for smolt. The upstream stocking of salmon that had begun as a "habitat study" has become a full-scale stocking effort above the dams.

Meanwhile the numbers of returning salmon have continued to be lackluster, even as stocking rates keep going up. Thirty-six reentered the river in 2001, forty-three in 2002 and again in 2003, and sixty-nine in 2004. There is still no explanation offered. Whatever it is that afflicts the fish, it is afflicting them everywhere, on both sides of the Atlantic, with the total number of sea fish being halved and then halved again in recent years.

In Maine, where the decline has been even more precipitous, the Atlantic salmon has been declared an endangered species, over the objections of both the governor and the Senate delegation, who fear more restrictions on timber and agriculture operations. Native salmon have always been returning to Maine rivers, and U.S. Fish and Wildlife Service argued for listing by claiming that Maine salmon are genetically distinct, while those who object to the listing say that such a genetic distinction is ridiculous after a hundred years of artificial breeding and stocking of hatchery fish.

Pacific Gas and Electric has been in quite a decline, too. After including a disclaimer on its e-mail correspondence for several years insisting that it was not the same Pacific Gas and Electric as the one in California, the fallout from the great energy speculation bubble seems to have caught up with it. After teetering on the edge for a while, the New England subsidiary has veered into bankruptcy court. The hydroelectric dams on the Connecticut are for sale again, and this time the probable buyer whispered about is an even bigger corporation from beyond the border. But it fears Vermont's "green" reputation, and there is a proposal in the Vermont legislature to buy the dams, giving power back to the people.

Meanwhile, the lawyers for PG&E are trying to negotiate the property taxes paid to local towns even lower. It will make the dams more attractive to a potential buyer, they say, as though local people already strapped by the escalation of property tax should be sympathetic. At least the hydro executives have moved out of their expensive offices in the business park. Now they're dispersed back to the little concrete rooms that had been originally built for them at the dams, or can be found in temporary construction huts nearby.

More mills are closing in the North Country, too. Ethan

Allen, the furniture manufacturer that has been capitalizing on that rock-hard name since 1937, closed its plant in Island Pond and laid off hundreds more in Orleans and Randolph, Vermont. CEO Farooq Kathwari said the consolidation was necessary to focus on more suitable plants. The plants are in China. Meanwhile American Tissue's former CEO Mehdi Gabayzadeh and accomplice Ali Amzad are finally facing federal charges of fraud. Their paper mills in Gilman, Vermont, and Berlin, New Hampshire, recorded twenty-five million dollars in phony sales and robbed the health care and pension accounts of hundreds of their workers before declaring bankruptcy. They left six hundred jobless and defaulted on their property taxes, crippling the local municipalities. With the help of accounting firm Arthur Andersen, it is said that they swindled investors out of three hundred million. Enron was about to buy them when that bubble burst, too.

When Kimberly-Clark decided to close the paper mill that has operated on the bank of the Connecticut in East Ryegate for more than a hundred years, it sent men into the plant with cutting torches to disable or remove the papermaking machinery. Spokespeople said they did it to eliminate the possibility of a competitor moving in, but it looked more like Sherman's march through Georgia and really means the impossibility of anybody reopening the plant at all. The shell of the plant, which employed almost a hundred people, recently sold for a hundred dollars. For the most part these stories — which are as scandalous as Enron and Global Crossing and have a much more powerful local impact — have been ignored in the local papers, which still think that business can do no wrong. And several local legislators still publicly insist that the mill closings are the result of Howard Dean's clear-cutting bill.

Back on the farm, things are even grimmer. While the price

of milk has remained fairly steady or climbed a bit in the supermarket, milk distribution has fallen into fewer and fewer hands, and now mostly belongs to Texas-based Sousa, with a few other big names dividing what is left. The price paid to farmers has fallen to what it was in the 1970s, while their costs have tripled. It is the same thing that is happening worldwide with the "consolidation" of other agricultural commodities such as cocoa and coffee, attended by the same wrenching social agony, loss, and dispersal.

In places the rural countryside is nearly deserted now. Some small towns in the South and the Midwest are empty: schools closed, churches closed. People who used to work on the farm, and then went to the mill when the farm failed, are finding the mills closing, too. So they join the rootless, finding work where they can, in the new wasteland we have created of asphalt and automobiles and housing tracts and shopping malls where everything looks the same no matter where on earth you are. The jobs are as disposable and transient as the workers are. We are more rootless than ever, more prone to whimsey and bellicose politics as the remaining roots are yanked out. Meanwhile in other, more fortunate rural places, where there are mountains for skiing or great beaches or scenic rolling hills, a blossoming new upper class is buying the old farms and ranches and turning them into private estates where they raise llamas and drive automobiles that cost more than most houses up here do.

Sometimes when I'm feeling morose I go down to the stream that lies at the foot of our farm. With a watershed of about twelve square miles, it has a pretty good flow in this last reach before merging with the Connecticut, and while there was once a road alongside it, at least six mills of various sorts, a covered bridge, and several small farms, that all went out in the great flood of 1927; the valley has lain largely deserted since then. The stream itself has resumed its timeless writhing through the floodplain, seeming undecided which way to go in a perfect miniature of what the floodplain valley of the great Connecticut once was like. It has reverted to what seems like chaos to many, but is in fact order of the highest sort: life in its greatest diversity and interdependence.

There are pools, deep and still, with great logs dipping down into them, and hatching insects rising into the air in swirling clouds. Beavers are at work; there is the pungent scent of freshly cut aspen.

There are bars of gravel, with the water chortling, great drifts of fine white sand, going to mud with the tracks of raccoons, deer, and coyotes. Tough, flood-beaten sedges cling to whatever footing they can find.

There are banks steadily being undercut where the water has changed its mind, with big sods of goldenrod falling in, and all the layers of clay and gravel and woody debris of thousands of years laid bare to see, weeping the red puss of iron oxide, where the water has changed its mind a hundred times before.

All of this lies below a sky unbroken by any sign of humankind, rimmed by the forest and silent but for the sound of the water itself. I like to wade, climbing over the bleached hulks of trees, feeling the textures of the land through my bare feet, the floodplain itself just at eye level. Here, a cloudy bit of glass worn smooth; there, the sole of a boot; otherwise it seems as it always was, although this, too, is an illusion. The slow crush of the glaciers, like death itself, put the big boulders in the bed — those chunks of hard granite, which doesn't even grow here — and before that, this was seafloor, and before that, nothing but star dust.

Now even the oceans are increasingly a reflection of ourselves. While the stocks of so many wild fish, not just the salmon, continue to plunge toward extinction, and coral reefs turn the skeletal white of death, there is speculation that we might use the oceans, where almost certainly life on earth originated. We could put the seas to work for us full time, like a vast lawn. Experiments have shown that the growth of green plankton, which is at or near the bottom rung of the evolutionary ladder, depends less on nutrients and sunlight than on the presence of iron oxide. Vast oceanic blooms of plankton are nourished in some places by the dust that blows from the continents and settles to the sea, while other parts of the ocean that are otherwise nutrient rich remain relatively sterile and barren. Experiments have already shown that we can stimulate green plankton blooms by spreading iron oxide from ships or airplanes. In turn, the plankton absorbs carbon dioxide from the atmosphere, which then rains down on the ocean floor as carbonate.

This would be good news for the energy sector, resonating though it does with the same jingoistic disregard for the consequences as the nuclear industry did in the 1950s. But for the speculative investors, it ups the feasibility of the next step, which would be to mine the vast stores of frozen methane theoretically awaiting us in the cold, dark depths. This "methyl ice" is estimated by some scientists to contain far more energy than all our reserves of coal, oil, and rock-bound natural gas by many times. It's hard to reach and tricky to extract, yes, and some scientists say that an upwelling of methyl ice was the cause of the Permian extinction. But explorations by American and Japanese companies have yielded some positive, though as yet expensive, results.

Then there's the fuel cell, which promises to make energy out of seawater itself, a startlingly sanguine claim that, as generally reported, ignores the energy required to separate that ancient and tenacious bond between hydrogen and oxygen in the first place. Well, some say we can use nuclear energy for that, so why bother to conserve now, when such a rosy future awaits us?

Meanwhile in Antarctica, the recent collapse of the Larsen A ice shelf was not accompanied by the sudden rise in the level of the ocean that some had predicted, for the shelf itself was already afloat anyway. But now the glaciers behind it are slipping toward the sea much faster — two meters a day at last measure, which is four times the previous pace — and the same thing is happening to the north, too. Soon the dream of a Northwest Passage from the Atlantic to the Pacific will come true. Some say this will be a windfall for maritime shippers, but cold fresh meltwater is also changing the balance of salinity and temperature that drives the global deep-ocean currents. It could shut off the Gulf Stream, plunging Northern Europe into an ice age while the rest of the planet swelters. Norwegian glaciers, which are fast disappearing, could come back in a hurry.

According to the Associated Press, the Inuit of the Canadian subarctic are already witnessing the most dramatic change. Rosemarie Kuptana in Sachs Harbor says winter comes a month later now. The permafrost is melting and the foundations of buildings are cracking; she's worried the village itself may someday slide into the sea on a sheet of mud. Meanwhile the polar bears are roaming inland, and it is difficult for the men to hunt seals, for the sea ice is no longer able to support them. As some native species suffer, other new ones are arriving. There are more beetles and sand fleas, and the mosquitoes are staying longer into the summer months. Birds such as robins and barn swallows are coming in spring now, and there are herring and salmon spawning in the streams. Perhaps these are the missing salmon.

It is midwinter now as I sit by the fire, and the walls of the otherwise darkened living room are bathed in flickering orange light. While our planet decides whether it may become less hospitable, more like Mars or Venus, the full moon is shining outside on rolling fields of snow. On a night like this, when it is so cold the trees crack like gunshots, and there is hardly more than a pane of glass between where I am and where I would quickly perish, it seems almost as though our earth has slipped its solar tether entirely and gone off on its own. But the moon has cast a square of pale light through the window and onto the living room floor, and there, with the square of moonglow as her stage, my bunny is dancing, dancing alone on her hind legs, forelegs pawing the air, dancing to a cosmic tune that only she can hear.